THE GOLD ARC
A Study of the Jewellery
Industry

SHANTANU RAJGURU

DEDICATION

To my grandfather (Late) Shri Shaktipada Rajguru,
an eminent writer, and my father (Late) Shri Benoy
Rajguru, who inspired me to pen down
my thoughts in this book

"Time is the coin of your life. It is the only coin you have,
and only you can determine how it will be spent.

Be careful lest you let other people spend it for you."

—Carl Sandburg

'The book is an excellent resource of Gold & Jewellery Industry in India. The reader is taken on a journey through the world of gold jewellery and its implications to modern day economy. The tone of the book reflects a learned appreciation for the marvel of this industry'.
Indrajit Ghosh, Ph.D, Financial Market Analyst.

'A compelling reminder of gold that plays a vital role in the Indian economy…..a fine account, neatly constructed and illuminating'.
Sanjay Singh, Sr. Director, GJEPC, India.

'Deep insights into the chemistry of jewellery sector exploring its great business perspective, a very interesting and a must read….'
Dhruba Jyoti Basu, Sr. Jt. Director, EEPC, India.

'The Gold Arc is very informative, represents current jewellery industry scenario from Hallmarking to marketing to promotion of business……Very useful for young

entrepreneurs, students, academicians and of course the jewelers.'
Rajeeb Bhusan Mukherjee, Professor, Management Science.

'Practical, informative book dealing with the gems and jewellery trade, gives an insight into the legalities of the trade and also the challenges of the future and dealing with these challenges in a legally profitable way.....'
Basudeb Acharya, Regional Director, LEEMUIR, Logistic Services.

'A thoughtful new book on gold and jewellery, portraying Indian jewellery industry challenges with reflections on where it will go in the next decade......could not be more timely.'
Soumitro Mukherjee, Businessman.

'Great reading. Very interesting, crisp, & fluid approach taken by the author to have a proper perspective on the functions of gold & jewellery in India and its future.'
Atanu Guha, Markeing Consultant, Pharmaceutical.

'This book has portrayed many issues on gold and jewellery that has never been compiled in such a systematic manner.'
Dibyendu Sinha Roy, FCA, Professional Consultant.

Contents

Gold the repressed Money ● India's Love for Gold ● Policy Journey of Gold ● London Gold fix Mechanism ● Price of Gold and its making ● Position of Gold in Indian Economy ● The Jewellery heritage that makes India proud ● India's approach to Export Policy ● Gold-a nuanced approach.

The Marketing matrix of Jewellers ● The future of manufacturing ● MSME schemes that languish for need of awareness ● The concept of Lean Manufacturing Technique ● The unique Wage payment model in India ● The idea of Hallmarking ● The Distribution channel in Jewellery industry ● Beneficial Ownership in the age of AML/CFT and the revenue model ● Indian way to deal with Financial Action Task Force ● The idea of preventing crime while increasing revenue ● The idea of VAT packed in the name GST • GST guidelines and its implications on Gold Jewellery in India.

The challenges that come from within • Doing business in India digitally • Jeweller's need to accommodate in the era of digitalization • Rating Agencies that rest on conflict of interest and unaccountability • The idea of rating the Rating Agencies • The coming opportunities in emerging markets • A glance at the future decade • Jewellery industry in 2020

ACKNOWLEDGEMENTS

I thought cf writing this book with the aim of keeping people aware about the sweeping changes that may overwhelm the future course of the jewellery industry in India in terms of policy interventions and technological developments that is all pervasive. First of all, my sincere thanks goes to The Gem and Jewellery Export Promotion Council, India, where I have worked for more than a decade. I am thankful to its employees and elected office bearers because of whom I got to understand much about the dynamics of Jewellery industry in India.

I am grateful to my 81A classmates of Denobili School, Dhanbad, and to my family for encouraging me to write on the challenging subject of gold and jewellery as against the current international settings, the emerging market concerns, which may affect our daily lives.

I am fortunate to have Souvik Majumdar who assisted in editing this book, Indranil Sanyal for his guidance and Siddharth Chakraborty for designing the cover, for which I am sincerely thankful. My invitations to discuss with friends, relatives, in social programmes and ofcourse internet have helped me to sharpen in contributing to this book. Some of my most valuable guidance came from friends and family who read early drafts of this book as everyday citizen and are equally concerned about the economy and the country.

I am indebted to Prof. Noam Chomsky, Dr. Ron Paul, James Rickard, David Stockman, whose exemplary body of works have inspired me immensely and I remain grateful to them.

Any work is usually collaborative in some way. There is rarely a manuscript that cannot be improved by good editing and I gracefully leave it to the readers to accommodate in case of any shortcomings. The greatest challenge had been time, which somehow I had to manage, and in completing this book if there are any mistakes I fully own it entirely.

My immediate family was a continuous source of support and encouragement. My daughter Garima for allowing me to filter and polish my thoughts through regular conversations, and my mother Pushpa who constantly kept disciplining me even today for working at odd hours at night and has kept me grounded. I am deeply indebted to my wife Santa for her love, care, support and continuous encouragement in writing this book who has always been a mirror for my understanding of the subject and for its refinement.

I am grateful to my entire family for their immense patience during my non participative domestic conversations and bearing with me. I love you all.

INTRODUCTION

This book is a compilation of current selected themes that struggle to make "Physical Gold" a replacement for Money even today. The book tries to connect some of the new regulatory and structural developments in the realm of financial matters that with digital technological interventions seems to be a distinct advantage in the future. My relationship with the Gem & Jewellery industry which accounts for more than a decade has led to many basic enquires that has continued to pester me about centrality of gold on the World Monetary Framework and the World Order few of which may include-Why central banks hold on to gold as reserve? What is gold's role and its function in the World Financial system? How is the price of Gold decided and who settles the price of gold? Why money that once anchored in gold had to go away? What is the requirement for gold price manipulation and what prompted introduction of paper gold? What is the significance of gold to person and what are its functions and uses? How do India oversee gold in a restrictive domain in perspective of its customary heritage and love for Gold and Jewellery objects? For what reason is the workmanship that include intricate designs in gold jewellery is influenced because of gold control measures? What decides every nation to take a position on gold? For what reason do nations structure their gold strategy according to their financial accommodation? What is the situation of gold in the Indian economy and what has been its policy approach? What are the components that decide India's gold policy since independence? For what reason is there a fine distinction that separates Indian way to deal with gold?

Countless enquires over a span of time with each new one originating every other day has made me curious about the fact that in the midst of all the natural inclination that influences gold supply in India, which being import dependent, how are the Indians able to deal with their tremendous hunger for gold and hand-made jewellery throughout the year? Some of the interesting questions about gold that is still an enigma to a common man some of which includes-How Indians are constrained to adjust and behave to hook on to its own jewellery legacy and magnificence? What sort of marketing mix, manufacturing techniques, distribution channels, unique loss-wage model of laborers, used for ensuring its old legacy of different jewellery types? Why hallmarking, a procedure for buyer insurance, took such a large number of years to take off in India? What is the eventual fate of manufacturing? What are the incentives accessible for MSME sector, a spine to Indian industry, which endured because of awareness insufficiency? What is the possibility of Lean Manufacturing technique? Why precious stones and metals, for example, gold been discovered a method of money laundering or tax evasion movement? What has prompted the structure of beneficial ownership and characterize legal person? Why have such a significant number of regulations shockingly overpowered the Indian economy with the regulation of structural changes like FATF, GST and what are its beginning? Does it have anything to do with raving up income? What are the difficulties that are to show with the appearance of digitalization in the economy? What sort of readiness really is required to fight the computerized intercession? What is the role of rating agencies in distribution of fund? What are the possibilities of the emerging markets and what does it hold for the future decade?

This book is simply an effort that tries to investigate, detail, examine and find answers to some of above mentioned questions in the form of essays and encourages curious others to investigate it further. Each of the expositions endeavors to scan for the inception of issues, make sense of the reason and the conceivable effect on the business, having some reference to precious metal gold jewellery. With an end goal of convenience and brevity, whatever have been talked about gold & jewellery is symptomatically material to silver and jewellery extensively, putting aside the relative market prices of silver and characteristic refinement in its applicability.

The general methodology has been to probe into the domestic strategies on gold that essentially is administered by the world multilateral institutions, for example, the International Monetary Fund (IMF) and the Bank for International Settlement (BIS). The intention is to bring into focus the role of gold in world geo-politics and its pertinence in the world fiscal and monetary framework. It also raises the basic issue as to-Why people won't go on with personal gold standards, understanding that men in power and banking elites have stopped discussing gold freely and overlooked it, while they themselves clutched it.

In the Indian setting, jewellery business is home to an exalted age-old heritage which India takes pride for its rich craftsmanship and specialty. It is usually positioned among the top three principal businesses in the nation from the export and employment point of view. It is well known that India does not mine or produce gold and is to a great extent an importer, but because of her gifted craftsmanship and workmanship, has been able to create her very own market.

The unsettled question in India is when both economic growth and stability, monetary development and security in the monetary system are fundamental concerns, is it not vital to locate the right balance between encouraging new growth and the way towards social inclusion?

In India people adore gold, and the gold and jewellery consumption is somehow attached to its way of life. For Indian women gold is considered as a noticeable social security incentive or particularly "Streedhan". Gold is always considered as an asset predominantly in rural areas where alternative means of storing value is constrained. This makes the gold and jewellery demand the biggest patron for the retail venture. The book presents certain selected topics that examines gold and its inherent properties and price appropriate for making jewellery. It also examines how the Central bank has been able to influence the market through setting up "Central Bank Gold Agreement" in 1999. Regardless of presentation and exercise of endless control measures in international and national gold strategy, Indians stay unflinching in gold and jewellery consumption passed on by its culture and rich heritage. It recognizes that gold supply in India is ruled by imports with little production locally that drives the recycled gold supply market in yearly gold consumption. The economic conditions decide the recycling activity in India, which is sensitive to gold price. The relationship of gold jewellery with weddings, commemoration, birthdays, especially during the festive seasons like "Diwali", "Christmas", "Akshay tritiya", "Dhanteras" to name a few where jewellery presents enlarges the celebration.

Further the book discusses about the Gold Control policy drawn to regulate gold supply, lessen smuggling, diminish demand for gold, decrease domestic price of gold and above all to move individuals away from gold. The Gold reserve was re-valued. The minimum reserve system pegged currency far from earlier proportional reserve system. The investigation analyzes the period from 1944 to 1963 when private gold holding, gold bonds, gold control

15

rules and acts, cancelation of gold control act 1990, harmonization with liberalization process in 1991, everything played out. This was followed by policies such as Special Imprest License, Gold under Open General License, Gold Deposit Schemes, Hallmarking, duty free import, and formulation of EXIM policy, Export processing Zones, Special Export Zones and the likes. Various national organizations and important bodies monitored and controlled the gold policy and trade through a structure for regulations, notifications and public notices, and examined the role and function of every division that featured independently. The new strategy on gold jewellery and its inputs have been talked about in terms of Export promotion policy.

The London Gold Fix Mechanism searches out-How the gold merchants and banks settle price, its historical mechanism, and how it changed over a period of time with most recent developments in LBMA dominated gold price fixing. How another electronic price-discovery mechanism is to supplant the long established London Gold Fix, implying that the gold benchmark will be set by means of an electronic platform overseen by the ICE Benchmark Administration including approach of Chinese bank in gold fix mechanism.

The price of gold and its making tries to clarify how dollar price of gold is inverse of the dollar, and how one can get a global point of view on gold in perspective of the cross-currency rates. It endeavors to reason why gold is thought of as a quantity by weight and physical holding, and not by the dollar price, which continues to change because of market manipulations. How the variation of demand and supply of gold influences both gold and paper markets in market making and different types of market manipulations.

The administration of demand and supply of gold has essential policy implications for fiscal and exchange rate management and ongoing mobilization of gold as budgetary instrument, has picked up consideration. The economic liberalization acquired critical changes in regulation governing purchase and ownership of gold. It takes a look at those aspects responsible for proposal of Gold Management Board. A series of events post independence and after economic liberalization, talked about gold policy initiatives of the government in present shape that incorporates recommendation offered by RBI to the administration in course of time. Recommendation offered on institutional development to mobilize gold and allow their use as financial asset in contrast with different nations. The need of forward trading in the era of liberalization analyzed in reference to other central banks in the world for the development of gold market and gold exchanges. It is seen that RBI and Government of India could assume a role in building up the gold market.

The book touches upon the various types of jewellery in India and takes a view on its magnificent legacy that transcends back to 5000 years. An article that cherish the different forms and objects covering the Antique, Bridal, Bead, Custom, Fashion, Filigree, Gold Jewellery, Ivory, Jadau, Kundan, Lac, Meenakari, Navratna, Pacchikam, Silver, Stone, Temple and Tribal Jewellery. The accentuation is much on handcrafted jewellery.

The book tries to comprehend India's way to deal with Export Policy and subtle elements of Indian trade policy, focused on self-reliance, adopted the strategy of import substitution and industrialization and developed a system of price controls and quantitative restriction. It also indicates the need to open ways for foreign participation through the process of liberalization and policy reforms to enhance productivity and competitiveness of Indian enterprises. A genuine endeavor has been made to comprehend the progression of FTP's and perceive the policy implications that decide the development in exports over a time of the Gem and Jewellery sector under different five years Foreign Trade policies. Gold has always been treated differently and approach towards it is continuously obscure. Overview demonstrates that there is a mobilization of world's gold from West toward the East. It alludes the role of gold in currency management, foundation of Shanghai Cooperation Organization, BRICS, and reset of world reserve currency and monetary standards.

There is a discussion on the procedures, publicity, advertising, marketing blends, strategies and plans that jewellery dealers employ to draw clients and build up loyalty. The article examines how jewellery retailers and actors work in competitive environment, that is influenced from conventional techniques to grasp latest offerings of branded jewellerys, exchange offers, financial facilities, transport facilities, lucky draws, celebration sponsorships, special offers, gifts, price discount, refreshments, individual attention and numerous different forms evolving frequently.

It peeps into the future of Jewellery manufacturing that dynamically changes and enhances in the circle of advanced innovations, digital technologies, CAD/CAM, rapid prototyping and manufacturing, precious metal alloy technology for unrivaled performance in manufacturing and finish when worn by clients. The eventual fate of manufacturing related to regular advances in technology is ready to rise.

A voyage made to the universe of different MSME schemes announced by government that are on offer for a wide range of jewellery practitioners alongside thoughts regarding different departments that are congenial, which are involved to actualize the important schemes. The idea of Lean Manufacturing Techniques (LMT) is a thought that MSMEs and SMEs may embrace for improvement in all segments of a manufacturing system. It is an integrated system approach where individuals' knowledge is basic to sustainability, comprehension and usage to enhance proficiency and profitability. The discourse infers that the dynamic knowledge opens up the way to innovation and adds to the development of the organization.

A typical form of wage payment technique in the gold and jewellery sector appears in wage-loss mechanism. The quantity, quality and assortment of the finished jewellery, considered three noteworthy determinants of the wage loss, swings in the same direction as that of relation with quantity produced. The foundation of this model has relieved the industrial relation challenges, and in some measures the dispute over wages, prompting significant gain in production capabilities, whereas very little gain showed in labor welfare, laborer's well-being, family, child-labour, education and their general working conditions.

An attempt has been made to bring into focus the origin of Hallmarking, which is a type of consumer protection and assurance, and how it advanced over a period of time in Europe and other parts of the world. It also underlines the necessities, laws, enactments and the difficulties of implementation in India.

The jewellery products put in the pipeline through marketing channel have been talked about primarily, and how different players move it along to the buyer toward the end of the channel. There are intermediaries that make the conveyance channel have various stages in the channel length for both domestic and exports. The related complexity in the pipeline relies on scope of capacities required for viability of the distribution channel, which relies on effective movement of products and its title from production to consumption.

The origin of Financial Action Task Force (FATF) that address Anti-Money Laundering (AML) and Combating Financing of Terrorism (CFT) are looked at to study the set standards for technical compliance and adequacy, ready with Beneficial Ownership and Legal Person ideas, which eventually is for tax reasons. The principles of FATF and India's readiness is assessed in its drive for AML/CFT measures and thus how the PMLA act 2002 is lined up with the provisions of the FATF have been dealt here.

Efforts have been made to see how Precious Metals and Stones (PMS) are alluring to criminals and utilized in AML/CFT. The proceeds of smuggling and corruption are laundered in Trade Based Money Laundering (TBML). A discourse made on 'Risk Based Approach' to PMS and the different provisions of FATF for general awareness. It uncovers how compliance for the PMS increases tax commitments and revenues especially with small taxpayers who are out of the framework.

A concise discourse on tax issues that require attention beyond electronic commerce as the VAT is potential to distort cross border trade in services and intangibles that make deterrents to business activity with distorted competition. An account of how OECD created International VAT or GST rules to reduce the vulnerability and risk of double taxation and non-taxation due to irregularities in VAT application across borders has been included. The standard for VAT treatment of most regular International transactions on trade in services and intangibles among partners is underlined. This exemplifies broad–based taxes on consumption collected from businesses through a staged collection process, yet not hypothetically to be borne by organizations, irrespective of the methodology whether Invoice credit approach or Subtraction technique. To make exports free of VAT systems that work on invoice credit method, the VAT on cross border business-to-business supplies of goods and services is collected by Reverse Charge Mechanism that switches the liability to pay the tax from the supplier to the customer, a way to collect more tax. The rules to GST extended widely that administer the jewellery trade in India and its entire pipeline including unregistered business entities and expand awareness.

There is a scan for issues that the gem and jewellery industry faces from within regarding the raw material supply, price volatility, source of capital, working capital, bank rates, transportation, skilled labor, infrastructure, changing design trends and preference and above all Research and Development. Insufficiency of all or some of these render organizations uncompetitive.

An examination has been made on foreign organizations that invest and acquire assets in India and the difficulties they face in the transforming digital space. It calls for learning the art of doing business in Indian way. It digs into procedures employable by global organizations for entering local markets against low price local partners. The emergence of a rising market to digital content and services that offer new opportunities in the digital marketing space through the internet sales channels that tries to change conventional promotion and advertising landscape to be more content driven. The requirement for selling provincial and local advertisement in local languages on cell phones for easy acceptability, clearness and comprehension that may evolve with easy to use content. Jewellery broadcast every day on a devoted website might be viewed as an entertainer in which Jewellery will be a piece of the story line.

With the rising non-performing assets, the role and function of rating organizations has been discussed to comprehend the revenue model of rating agencies, and assessed how it might influence the rating decisions and conflict of interest, rating shopping by the corporate to gain better evaluations. The institutional reaction post 2008 crisis, driven by G20, advocate strong oversight over rating agencies through sets of accepted rules, that meet highest standards that try to offer greater divulgence to investors and issuers, especially separating complex financial related instruments. Attempt has been made to analyze the CRA activities in Indian setting and how the revenue model and business competition influence routinely the decision procedure of the CEOs. The article examines fundamentally a portion of the perspectives and the path forward.

A fresh look at the oncoming opportunities in emerging markets reveal that another consumer class is fast developing in the digital age with more number of users. The electronics and white goods industries may drive the global demand in focusing growth. Clusters may compete with low price local players in the era of digital revolution. An integrated digital campaign strategy may build brand and trust across a range of channels. The growth will originate from large number of customers who try new products.

A look at the future decade discusses the jewellery market in emerging markets ready to grow and alter the economics of manufacturing. The ethical source of precious metals and gems may assume a dominant role later on as the idea of 'green jewellery' that gets in the price chain from mines to market pipeline. The push for accreditation schemes for gold and diamond may grow. Recycling activity, use of safe materials, superior finish, and tarnish resistant, unusual colours might be the new frontiers of growth The hollow casting technology may offer exploration with RPT and direct casting of resin models. The improvements in investment machine technology and its consumables, rubber moulds and investment powders are for the most part holding up to spread wings.

Jewellery industry in 2020 studies the charges that are in progress both in consumer behavior and in the business itself. The procedures of internationalization and consolidation, development of branced products, reconstructed distribution channel, hybric consumption, fast fashion likely to capture the imagnation of the consumers. The branded jewellery segment may use digital media platforms relaying information data, shaping brand identity, and customer relationships and how single brand stores that have more control of their brands and contacts with shoppers, is probably going to pick up in comparison to the multi brand boutiques or departmental stores.

CHAPTER 1

Philosophy of Gold and Jewellery

☐ Gold the repressed money

I

t is often said by authorities that for the sake of national interest, limit the gold import and decrease trade deficit while one appears not to have alternatives in oil, edible oil, coal, capital merchandise or any other. Indians have been asked to deposit physical gold in banks yielding 2.5 percent interest that might be utilized for supply to jewellery dealers, as a substitute for import. At the same time, gold backed bond in paper was announced that later could be en-cashed at an equivalent price. Coins were issued carrying the World Gold Council name for authentication of the scheme. The extent to which the public or the religious community showed enthusiasm for the scheme is anybody's guess given the off take of the scheme wherein just 400 gms were lifted in a fortnight after the declaration of the scheme in 2015, which is insignificant. What the media speculates in the hesitation of individuals to declare assets for tax implications may hold some truth, yet the question that comes up is whether it is a case of deficit trust in government? Establishment depict trade deficiency as private sector issues, however private sector always pays for its goods when imported. Does it imply that trade shortfall is always a result of government intervention and money related inflation? Is it that Gold import being only responsible a misplaced propaganda? Does government need individuals' savings for its own purpose and acquire physical gold for paper? Why is public gold procurement considered hoarding of assets beyond government reach? It has been referred to as import came to over 1000 tons in 2012 and the duty imposed gradually to 10 percent. This coincided with the appointment of a new Governor of RBI, who is a strong believer of de-regulation, and who could be credited with monetary policy reducing price inflation and economic progress. The governor, central to re-imposition of control on gold, appear to be conflicting with his de-regulation principles. Is there a need to comprehend this logical inconsistency in key global context? Is it not that the Western banks were worried of the growing interest of gold by China and India where the combined populace of 2.5 billion are absorbing gold more than mines and scrap recycling aggregate, depleting the European vaults prompting emergency in capital markets? Did the strong domestic demand for gold and the prohibitive policy stance reflect in the higher price of gold in the domestic market compared to international prices that create a spread for activating smuggling? Has the time come to recognize that gold is money ? "The value of gold comes from the market place and governments can't reproduce the gold, unlike paper currency, which gets its value by government declaration and printed at will" as noted by Dr. Ron Paul, eminent author, congressman and US Presidential candidate in 2008. It is proven, times immemorial that gold is a form of money. It is gold that preserves wealth in case of financial volatility and downturn and act as a safe haven. Had it not been so, the central bank or sovereign governments worldwide would not have held tight to gold reserve of around 35,000 tons even today of the estimated above surface 170,000 tons of gold worldwide, which is around 20 percent of aggregate gold available. In this arrangement, India's household and sanctuaries are estimated to preserve 22,000 tons of gold. This is 17 percent of the remaining above ground gold of which our central bank RBI has around 558 tons. This is around 1.7 percent of the aggregate central banks holding that offers a compelling argument for gold as a store of significant value. Have we at any point asked this question to the authorities that decide gold control in the country? At one hand sovereign governments cover its risks holding on to gold and at the same time it discourages and conveys a notion to its people to relinquish gold in any form. It is realized that India has large stocks of gold which is extremely hard to prioritize, like a preferred form of wealth to women, religious, ceremonial and as a hedge to inflation, however we can safely conclude on its combined impact. From available indications, 80 percent goes into jewellery fabrications including around 10 percent for exports, 15 percent for investor demand (depends upon economic buoyancy in the domestic market) and remaining 5 percent might be for industrial use. The question that normally emerges from our frame of discussion that does not always meet our eyes precisely is the role and function of gold in the realm of geopolitics and for what reason is there a mobilization of gold from West towards the East? What role gold might play in currency management, the game plan in Shanghai Cooperation Organization, BRICS, and in so far as that is concerned the reset of world reserve currency? Is it just domestic policy that decides gold control or is it intervention of supranational institutions like BIS , IMF and Federal reserve that administer gold movements? Especially in Indian setting and century old practices, gold is used in jewellery, which is visually alluring and pleasing to the wearer, and is considered a wearable wealth, then why is it not worth to be given attention when such large number of individuals are employed and make a living in this industry?

To comprehend the role of gold in the world, there is a need to understand the function it plays in the world monetary framework after the formation of central banking system in 1913. Towards the beginning of WWI around 1914, the world monetary system was tied to classical gold standards. Nations entering the war gradually moved away from gold standard so that they could finance the war with enhanced credit borrowing. (London was the focal point of the then worldwide finance and pound sterling the benchmark reserve currency). Post war, Winston Churchill wanted to come back to gold standard and at pre-war price (Pound 2.45 per ounce) while Sir John Maynard Keynes, the famous British economist, thought of it as deflationary that provoked him to state, "Gold is a barbarous relic". He wanted the price of gold to reset. Nevertheless, Winston Churchill still held on to pre-war price of gold standard, which did not permit addition of extra liquidity in the economy and considered it in substantial measure to have caused the Great Depression. From that point onwards "gold is a barbarous relic" has turned into a much practiced recital of those individuals who posed confidence on paper money and hence focussed on upholding it and not gold. Despite the fact that J.M.Keynes, contended for another type of currency at Bretton Woods in 1944, to be specific, "Bancor", the hypothetical ancestor to Special Drawing Right (SDR), yet in this manner, USA did push for dollar-gold standard that kept going from 1944 to 1971. The interest groups favoring paper money took a slightly different view of gold as a "primitive relic", though, Sir. J.M.Keynes, in his early vocation supported gold standard, in the middle of his profession upheld reset price of gold, and later again pushed for gold standard, as observed by economists

In the year 1971, President Nixon, through an executive order rejected gold standard to bring forth fiat dollar currency propped up by petro dollar that proceeded until 2011. Post 2008 financial crisis, dollar as fiat currency has confronted severe test because of excessive printing of paper dollar to fuel growth. The growth stayed subtle, despite of Quantitative Easing's (QEs) and low interest regime; driving Central bankers to institutionalize the process of alternative reserve currency, Special Drawing Right (SDR), backed by five principal currencies in the basket in addition to gold. A few nations began trading outside of the dollar system and in currencies backed by gold, because of shifting geopolitical situation towards east. The countries put under sanction began trading in lieu of gold (e.g. Iran). This clearly proves that gold is still considered as money.

Today, the money in digital form are nothing but electrons that store digits, which don't rust and are not rare, which are in silicon chips. This can easily be hacked and deleted. In contrast, the gold atoms are by far stable and cannot be hacked or erased by cyber brigade. Indeed, even in the digital age, gold still stands as money. Digital wealth is again prone to power blackouts, infrastructure or exchange collapses. Some commentators see that gold has no yield, no return, no compounding wealth and henceforth not an investment product. Without a doubt, it has no yield since it has no risk, yet again gold has yield when monetary policy drift towards the negative interest territory (e.g. Japan). Gold that is purchased and kept today might stay intact in as much as its price changes, which is the problem of the currency that is paired with gold. Since gold has no issuer, hence it is no one's obligation and above all, no commodity risk involved when gold in physical form is considered. Gold again is not a commodity as it does not have much of industrial use, or input to any production process, apart from some use in electronics among other examples. In any case, gold is traded in commodity exchanges, though not a commodity, since that development that influence commodity does not really affect gold. During Great Depression, most of the commodity prices were down, economy was in deflation, and furthermore industrial product output reached its nadir. Overall, in between 1929 to 1933, the US dollar price of gold remained fixed at 20.67 per ounce. In this case the gold played out the role of money and not as a commodity. The government raised the price to dollar 35 for each ounce to cause inflation. Today, the governments again fear for deflation and desire for inflation to reduce genuine burden of sovereign debts. Again, gold is not paper. The paper contracts made by London Bullion Market Association (LBMA) in Exchange Traded Funds (ETFs), in which case some gold is there at some place in the structure, yet nobody owns it. ETF's are only share of stocks and the structure that is really legitimate is the "trust" that the Trustees have in some form of physical gold at some place in some vault. Again, the shares in digital form can be hacked and erased. Moreover, if for any reason there should arise a of demand shock or buying panic for gold, the price of gold would rise substantially, in which case the paper contract may collapse without adequate backing of gold, as observed by James Rickard, a renowned author and advisor in international economics.

These contentions only prove that gold never went away. The men in power and banking elites quit discussing gold and thereby openly overlooked it, but they themselves held on to it. Had gold been so worthless, why would USA hang on to 8000 tons, Euro zone 10783 tons, Germany and IMF 3000 tons each, and for what reason would China procure 1000 tons every year if they do not see gold as equivalent of money and as an ideal instrument of hedge? The above stated facts guide us to seek for answers why jewellery that is produced using gold, which has a subjective value to its wearer, would not be advanced? Why is it only the privilege of central banks to purchase gold as reserve to hedge against risks? Why in absence of official gold standards, individuals would not go on a personal gold standard by purchasing gold or jewellery to protect wealth?

Especially, in the Indian context, jewellery business is home to a radiant age-old legacy and India takes pride in its rich art, workmanship and craft. It is positioned among the top three industries in the country as far as export and employment is concerned. It is known that India does not mine or produce significant gold and is generally import based, but because of its gifted artisans and workmanship that has enabled it to make a market of its own. Does it not become imperative for the government to guarantee lasting supply of the rare asset in the open market for development and sustenance of the industry? If gold import against total countries import is only found responsible for increased Capital Account Deficit (CAD), which drives government to increase tariff rates to reduce consumption, then that must have been reversed with the falling oil prices, calling for reduced import tariff that could spare jobs and arbitrary employee migration throttling the industry and its growth today. Would not there be immediate setback in the process of transforming family owned businesses to organized manufacture that might produce doubts in the minds of entrepreneurs for renewed investment in the industry? Since India is a huge market and values traditional gold jewellery are created by skilled craftsmen, how would the industry scale upwards without an unhindered supply of raw material, new enterprise and investments, and retrained labour force with new skills? Where would the sophisticated value addition be ? As innovation becomes key to progress in coming years with trends like Make in India, development of new brands, the establishment of clusters, Common Facility centres are necessary and supply side constraints are required to be eliminated. The products and services can thus become competitive both locally and internationally. Only when quality supply source is ensured, it might discourage informal trade across borders and potentially remove the possibility of raw material corruption. At a time when economic growth and financial stability are the must-have, it is to find the right balance between encouraging new growth and a way to reach social inclusions against restrictive trade policies.

☐ India's love for gold

"In the absence of gold standard, there is absolutely no way of protecting the savings from confiscation through inflation. No store of value. Shortfall in spending is simply a scheme for the confiscation of wealth. Gold stands in the way of this insidious process as a "protector of property rights" as said Alan Greenspan in 1966.

India's love for gold originates from the gold jewellery consumption, which is attached to its culture in the wedding related demand as gold, a metal that plays a fundamental role in wedding ceremony. "Streedhan" is often considered as most liquid and tradable investment for accumulation of wealth. Indians are drawn towards gold jewellery because of awareness of the consumers about gold's unique property of hedging and store of value. The demand for Indian jewellery accounts on an average 23 percent of world's jewellery demand. Generally, demand for gold jewellery is the largest contributor that represents 59 to 65 percent of retail investment space and remaining originates from industrial demand. The demand is often affected by the monsoon rain and in the performance of the farm sector of the economy that offer superior returns and income in the rural areas, where alternative means of storing value is constrained. It is known that most of the gold supply is from imports. The cross currency and swap rates between US dollar and Indian rupees decide the landing cost of gold, and any weakness in the rupee versus dollar makes the price of gold exorbitant.

The unmistakable qualities of gold, appropriate for making jewellery, are its ductile and malleable nature that render a single ounce equivalent to 31.104 grams. Just that bit can be drawn into a wire 35 miles in length and hammered into sheets under 5 millionth of an inch thickness, to the extent that gold foil appears translucent. Melting of gold at 1064.18 degree Celcius with a specific gravity of 19.30, it is viewed as the densest of metals that makes it to be a good conductor of heat and electricity, besides being a good reflector of light. Royal families in yesteryears used mirrors made of gold. The relatively chemically inert property of gold besides silver and platinum makes it a Noble metal, are precious because of its scarcity and durability. Gold is traded as refined gold bullion of purity in the range of 995 to 999 fineness. The London Bullion Market Association (LBMA) for 'good delivery bars' fits in with the International specification of 12.44 kilograms (400 ounces) of 995 minimum purity, carries a serial number that have good appearance and regular shape that bears the stamp of the approved smelters. The Kilo bars are preferred in Europe, Middle East and Asia, with 5 and 10 tola bars traded in India and Middle East. There are three primary sources of gold that originate from mines, recycled gold and official sector sale

33

of gold. Generally, the mine supply is 60 to 70 percent of aggregate supply. The mining includes gold production from primary deposits and secondary deposits are recouped as a by-product from other mining activities. The recycled gold from old scraps that make 33 percent of the aggregated gold supply is recovered from fabrication products, melted, refined and cast into bullion bars for resale. At whatever point there is an increase in gold price, supply of recycled gold increases, which is evident amid the economic volatility and difficult condition. Typically, recycled gold supply is in the region of 1800 tons. The official sector like Central Bank sales and IMF supply average around 300 to 400 runs occasionally to re-balance reserve asset between 1988 to 2009. This selling halted the 2008 crisis when advanced nations stopped selling and developing nations began purchasing in the midst of economic uncertainty. Furthermore, in the Bretton Woods conference in 1944, the gold standard helped the establishment of International fixed exchange rate regime in which currencies were pegged to US dollars and gold was $35 per troy ounce. At the point when this plan stalled, it set in motion the balance of payment problems. In November 1961, the London gold pool was set up by a group of eight Central banks, comprising of US and European nations that participated in keeping up the Bretton wood system of fixed rate convertible currencies while defending a gold price of $35 per troy ounce in the London gold market. Because of low gold pegged price in 1968, France pulled back from the gold pool to keep running, which brought about free-float of gold price. In 1971, USA needed to deliver 17000 tons of gold out of its hold to settle the balance of payment against European Nations. This, prompted suspension of gold convertibility for the US Dollars that reduced USAs reserve, which almost brought about a breakdown in the Bretton Woods' system. The Smithsonian Agreement in 1971 formed among the group of 10 major nations to revise the Bretton Woods Agreement, failed as well. This brought forward the floating exchange rate system, advanced by USA and followed by rest of the world that evolved losing some sheen from 'gold as reserve asset'. When it was observed (in mid 1990s) that inflation had gone, the nations started lessening their gold reserves to generate more returns and ended up as official suppliers of gold. In September 1999, Central Bank Gold Agreement (CBGA-1) was set up to restrict the yearly sales of gold in the next five years to 400 tons every year, with a ceiling of 2000 tons and this was concurred by all the European Central Banks alongside 14 other countries. CBGA-2 was conducted between 2004 to 2009 to increase yearly limit to 2500 tons, followed by CBGA-3 in September 2009 with a yearly ceiling of 400 tons planned and oriented to accommodate IMF program of limited gold sales. Gold deals by European Banks fundamentally reduced against looming debt crisis as gold assets found to offer predominant gains as the value of gold increased.

Despite a few changes presented in the international policy combined with the exercise of incalculable control measures, the craving for gold jewellery consumption by the Indians always remained unaffected for the sheer love of yellow metal that was passed on by its culture and rich legacy.

☐ Policy journey of Gold

The Government of India is known to monitor the import, export, distribution, fabrication, retailing, and private ownership of gold since 1947. The gold control policy has been drawn to regulate the gold supply, reduce smuggling, lessen demand for gold, diminish domestic price of gold and above all to move individuals away from gold. The degree of regulation of the gold industry had changed that reflects in the policy embraced by government post independence. In 1947, import and export of gold or bullion were restricted under Foreign Exchange Regulation Act (FERA) of 1947. The official holdings of gold reserve of Reserve Bank of India (RBI) revalued with minimum reserve system to currency against the earlier proportional reserve system. From 1944 to 1963, the private ownership of gold and operation of domestic gold industry were confined. To mobilize immense reserve of gold in the country, in November 1962, a 15 years Gold Bond at the rate of 5 to 6 percent interest was issued (for gold, coins and ornaments), which got 16.3 tons. This was combined with urging public to avoid purchasing gold and surrender their holdings to government and approach banks to call for advance loan against gold. Forward trading was forbidden at that point. In January 1963, Gold control rules were introduced and the final provisions enacted under Gold Control Act in September 1968. The domestic gold market was additionally controlled as the private gold possession was restricted to gold jewellery wherein gold coins were already in circulation. Owning gold bars became unlawful. License was required by Gold jewellery fabricators to work and was regulated. The limited bar and medallion producers were precluded. The refiners of old gold scraps couldn't refine without approval and were closed. The bullion merchants generally stopped trading at least officially. The makers of new jewellery had to rely on recycling of gold scraps and were restricted to making gold jewellery of more than 14 carats purity. Another endeavor was made in 1965 to collect gold with a new series of Gold Bond at the rate 7 percent that raised 6.1 tons. The third series, National Defense Gold Bond, was issued in 1980 that fetched 13.7 tons redeemable in Gold of standard purity at maturity, unlike the earlier one repayable in Rupees. The value of gold determined was dependent on international price. The voluntary disclosure of Income and

Wealth Amended Ordinance in 1975 allowed immunity to all disclosures of wealth, income and gold within a stipulated time. The Government's strong disapproval in smuggling operation and as a major aspect of financing the deficit budget plan 1978-79, was considered to act as anti-inflationary measure, when gold was auctioned to bring around 1050 crores. This strategy received extreme criticism and was withdrawn in October 1978. In June 1990, the Gold Control Act was revoked as it became obvious that the business went underground and since then unofficial import became relentless with high gold premium in the domestic market. The cancellation of Gold Control act harmonized well with the new National policy of liberalization of the economy in 1991. By March 1992, merchants were no longer required to work under license and the private ownership of gold fell. The Non Resident Indians (NRI) were permitted to import gold up to 5 kilogram every six months, which increased to 10 kilograms by January 1997. The customs duty initially applied at the rate of rupees 450 for each 10 grams was later reduced to rupees 220 by April 1997. The NRI import during this period went up to 1249 tons, which later diminished. In April 1994, Special Imprest License (SIL) appeared that enabled exporters to utilize a portion of their overseas earnings to import specified products. The gold import was included and the license was tradable, which could be sold to domestic entities for their own import purpose. Under SIL scheme, 150 tons of gold bars, jewellery and medallion were imported, and in April 2001 the scheme was withdrawn with the introduction of Open General License (OGL) in November 1997. At first, under OGL seven banks were approved which was expanded to 20 and above. In 1993, Gold Bond of 5 years were issued that brought in 41.0 tons followed by Gold Deposit Scheme(GDS) wherein in 1991 State Bank of India was authorized to receive gold from public to earn 3 to 4%

interest in lieu of their deposits. Banks were allowed to use gold after due process of refining and for domestic jewellery manufacture. This GDS was allowed to five more banks and did not have limitations like 1962, 1965, 1993, and continued outgrowing. For improvement in quality, in the year 2000, Bureau of Indian Standards (BIS) started the certification scheme for Hallmarking of Gold Jewellery. In the initial two years 12 hallmarking Centres provided service to 275 certified jewellers rooted in 9 cities. In the export front of gold jewellery, since 1978, SBI was allowed to import gold free of duty for fabrication of jewellery, and consequently public sector units like HHEC (1982), MMTC(1989) STC(1997) were also permitted to import. To support these duty-free imports, several schemes were defined in Export Import (EXIM) policy by Government of India. To encourage export products including jewellery, Export Processing Zones (EPZ) were set up in 1980s and later in 2000 SEEPZ was changed over to SEZ status, where significant level of gold jewellery for export was fabricated.

The gold industry is monitored and controlled by a structure comprising of regulations, notifications, and public notices of a few government organization and bodies that are entrusted to do so by Ministry of Finance, Ministry of Commerce and Industries, Ministry of Consumer Affairs, Ministry of Coal and Mines, Reserve Bank of India and others. The Ministry of Finance is concerned about economic and financial related matters that influences the nation through the Department of Expenditure, Department of Revenue and Economic Affairs. The Central Board of Excise and Customs (CBEC) entrusted with formulating policy relating to levy and collection of Customs and Central Excise duties come under Department of Revenue. CBEC serves as the administrative authority for subordinate bodies like Customs and Central Excise, which screens and collects duties and guarantees that gold is officially not imported outside EXIM policy. The Department of Economic Affairs monitors and formulates the nation's economic policy and programs at the more extensive level. The banking division, having interest in gold related activities of banks, is concerned about working of Indian banking system. The mint that manufactures gold bars and medallions is under administrative control of Ministry of Finance. The Reserve Bank of India (RBI), setup in 1935 under RBI Act of 1934, was nationalized in 1949 under Banking Regulation Act 1949, which goes about as monetary authority for direction and supervision of the financial system, issues currency and oversees exchange control through its 22 provincial offices spread across state capitals. In RBI, Department of External Investment and Operations monitors official gold reserve, and co-ordinates meetings of the standing committee on gold. Department of exchange control looks matter relating foreign exchange and Department of Banking Operation and Development (DOBOD) is associated with the authorization and monitoring of the banks in public and private sectors that import gold and operates gold schemes. The standing committee on gold and precious metals in RBI advises the government on National Gold Policy and is represented by authorities of Ministry of Finance and Commerce and Industries. Historically, however, licensing and regulating were within the domain of RBI. However, in 1992, after the amendment of Foreign Exchange Regulation Act (FERA)1973, gold import and export fell under the domain of national EXIM policy. It is to be understood that government is associated through several institutions, either completely or partly, in the activities of gold and commerce. The public sector banks, public sector undertakings, Bureau of Indian Standards, Nationalized Gold Mining Organizations and Indian government mints are on the whole fundamental part to the business activities

39

of gold. The Ministry of Commerce and Industry comprises of Department of Commerce, Department of Supply and Department of Industrial Policy and Promotion. The Directorate General of Foreign Trade (DGFT) is responsible for policy and regulations. It identifies the import and export of gold under EXIM policy, and controls the SEZs and EPZs, where jewellery is fabricated. It supervises the Gem and Jewellery Export Promotion Council (GJEPC) and different Public Sector Units (PSUs), self-ruling bodies occupied with gold related activities like MMTC, STC, HHEC and it comes under the control and supervision of the Ministry of Commerce. The Directorate of Commercial Intelligence and Statistics (DGCIS) that coordinates in gathering of import/export statistics, including gold, is under the authoritative control of Ministry of Commerce. In this arrangement, Handloom and Handicraft Export Council (HHEC), however dynamic in gold, falls under Ministry of Textiles. The BIS that propelled the certification scheme for hallmarking of Gold jewellery in April 2000 and which can approve independent companies to act as Assaying and Hallmarking Centres for the use of Jewelers as certified Jewelers, work under the large administrative control of the Ministry of Consumer Affairs, Food and Distribution. The Indian Bureau of Mines (IBM), which is under the control of Department of Mines, in the Ministry of Coal and Mines, operate the liberalized National Mineral Policy 1993 that encourages exploration and mining of gold.

The new Gold Control Act enacted in 1968 considered gold market participants into five categories that are public, licensed refiners, certified goldsmith, licensed dealers, and registered offices all of whom were controlled by Gold Control officers based in 30 collectorate across the country. The general public were permitted to buy gold 'ornaments' only, and not bars or any other forms, and individuals were required to declare their ownership of holding that exceeds 2 (two) kilograms or 4 (four) kilograms per family, and any change in ownership required notification to the authorities. The licensed refiners were restricted to melting, refining, assaying and making of bars for trade only but detailed records of all such transactions were required to be submitted to the authorities. This resulted in closures of all major refineries by 1989, barring few, which operated primarily to melt and assay gold Further, only self-employed individuals were certified to operate as certified goldsmith who could buy gold bars from licensed refiners or dealers, who could receive gold from them and public but not buy or sell jewellery and articles mainly of gold. They were not permitted to repair or polish any jewellery and were reduced to simply contract workers to dealers in reshaping old gold jewellery. The dealers were those entities who were engaged in buying or selling gold or gold jewellery among the trade actors including public, although most of them were jewellery retailers. Wholesalers and manufacturers involved in gold business in someway and employed artisans, were licensed as dealers but were allowed to conduct operation only within their own premises specified in the license. They could own gold bars from licensed refiners, but were subjected to quantity restriction to a maximum of 400 grams if they employed one artisan, rising to a maximum of 2 (two) kilograms for employment of more than 20 artisans. During this period all transactions and movements of gold required maintenance of official records so much that carrying samples became oppressive in the hands of bureaucrats. Here, the registered artisans were considered as a person employed or used by licensed dealers but not by a certified goldsmith, to manufacture gold jewellery. The outcome of the Gold Control Act 1968 and several other measures limited gold jewellery products to handmade jewellery. The control measures allowed the industry to go underground, and transaction flourished in the use of cash and most of the transactions were conducted beyond official records. The number of Gold jewellery outlets were reduced as obtaining license became increasingly difficult giving rise industry fragmentation. The unorganized large jewellers could not grow and operations from single location prohibited them in the development of chain retail outlets, managed by a family member, who was still required to obtain chain license with individual right. These measures were counter to establishment of large jewellery factories and inhibited development of national wholesale companies, giving rise to small family owned businesses. As gold could only be owned as jewellery, and not bars, it became a vehicle of investment, particularly in absence of any other investable financial product understood by the rich farmers of rural India. The crude jewellery, like simple rings and bangles, apart from well-crafted jewellery, were fabricated for sale at low mark-up for investment as money. As the strict control regime gave rise to unofficial imports that was almost half the price on top of international price of gold, public passion to own gold reinforced and owning large quantities became the aspiration of public to protect their savings during the time of high inflation and Indian rupee devaluation.

With the turn of the liberalization of the Indian economy and with the annulment of the Gold Control Act 1990, to lend thrust to exports of jewellery from the country and consolidate the local market, getting of license was never again required relative to quantity of gold held. The industry saw development and extension prospects, which got accelerated with normalization of policy initiative by the successive governments in its follow through of five-year plans and amendments of Exim policy. There were some outstanding activities taken up by the government through duties, taxes, infrastructure grants towards expanding the capacity for export of Gem and Jewellery from the country. This was done by means of embracing liberal policies and procedures incorporated in Foreign Trade Policy (FTP) throughout the years and continuously refreshing and reforming it in a state of harmony with global standards. The evolution of trade policy augmented the idea of a SEZs and EPZs and upheld it with export friendly duty exemption policies to be successful With a few revisions and refinements of progressive FTP the duty incidence on gold and jewellery export were neutralized and duty drawback on such exports permitted. Duty free import entitlement for rejected jewellery was allowed at the rate of 2 percent free on board of turnover of previous year. The number of days for re-import of such items for participation in exhibition to US increased to 90 days. The value limit of individual carriage was increased to S 5(five) million for Overseas exhibition participation, and the rest US Dollar 1 million for fare advancement. Government also permitted 100 percent foreign direct investment in Gem and Jewellery Industry through automatic route to encourage more investment in the segment.

The component of jewellery include gold, silver, diamond, platinum, precious and semi precious stones mounted on to jewellery, aside from gold jewellery, and the fragmented industry generally fell into unorganized sector and is named Micro Small Medium Enterprise (MSME) industries. Right now the MSME unorganized sector players utilize indigenous technology that presents opportunity for strong growth prospects with enhancement in technique for production and use of superior technology and in this manner might scale-up that could add to economic growth The favorable policy regime that offers zero duty for procurement of rough diamonds, an import based item. The Pradhan Mantri Kaushal Kendras were introduced in more than 600 districts all over the nation. Skill Council of India for creating skills for the Gem and Jewellery sector was also introduced. The FTP 2015-2020 aims to help services and exports and liable to support the "Make in India" initiative. The Policy offers a critical regulatory framework for Special Notified Zones. The gold monetization scheme built up in November 2015 might empower people, Trusts, Mutual Funds to deposit gold with banks and earn interest on the same that require refinement. The Common Facility Centres (CFC) offers common basic pool to cutting edge machineries, hardware and equipment at less expensive rate to MSME precious stone manufacturers, coming up in Gujarat, however its utility depends on the characteristics and maturity of the production Centres encompassing it. Throughout the years government has supported different projects and undertakings that has been brought about by the industry in organizing International exhibitions and Fashion Shows. It has also broadened support for the establishment of a Jewellery Park with INR worth of 50 crores at Mumbai to move nearby handcrafted jewellery manufacturing factories to an ecological friendly development of trade and improved way of life. The presentation of GST by government has realized significant changes in the structure and its dynamics of tax administration that captures all the tax based on principle of place and supply of consumption whose treatment has been done in another article in this book.

☐ London gold fix mechanism

Historically, the gold fix mechanism involves gold dealers from London's five biggest bullion banks, which establishes a common transaction price for a large pool of purchase and sale order. They do this twice each business day at 10.30 am (Morning fix) and at 3.0 pm (Afternoon fix). The participating bullion banks act both on their own behalf and for their customers who have issued limit orders for them to trade at London Gold Fix Price (LGFP). A limit order is an order that sets the maximum or minimum price at which a participant is willing to buy or sell. It is designed to offer more control over buying and selling prices of the trade, has the advantage of entry and exit at specified asset price, thinly traded, highly volatile, and has a wide spread. This is like putting a ceiling on the amount an investor is willing to pay. Often limit orders are put in queue waiting for subsequent trading session to resume.

The gold fix establishes the price at which the gross amount of gold on buy-orders matches the gross amount of gold on sale-orders across all the participating banks. The gold fix Chairman starts the fixing process by declaring normally a price very near to the ongoing spot market gold price . Assuming this price, the participating banks aggregate all the limit orders they receive and sell and declare to the Chairman the net quantity of gold they would buy or sell, at the proposed price. If the net effect of all the participating banks is in balance, then that price becomes the LGFP. If incase the buyers and sellers are not immediately in balance, then the Chairman adjusts the proposed price upwards if too many buyers or downwards if too many sellers. An upward price adjustment would cause the prospective Gold Fix Price to exceed some of the purchase order limits that causes some orders to drop out of the pool and has reducing demand. While the prospective Gold Fix Price, when exceed some of the sale order limit, then it causes some orders to come into the pool and has increasing supply. A downward price adjustment would cause the prospective Gold Fix Price to drop below some of the purchase order limits, which will cause to include those orders in the pool that has increasing demand. Similarly, the prospective Gold Fix Price can drop to below sale order limit that causes those orders to drop out of the pool and has decreasing supply. The banks will use the adjusted price to repeat this process until they reach a balance. Thus a large pool of orders overhanging the market will be executed at a common price. Since the method involves a large pool, hence the perceptions of those who buy and sell gold through London Gold Fix consider it a Fair Auction Method. In this entire process, there exists a small spread of about 20 cents per troy ounce in premium and when applied on the fix price to buyers; it helps the participants to earn some money that keeps the fix momentum going. The five members are Bank of Nova Scotia-Scotia Mocatta, Barclay Bank, Deutsche Bank, HSBC USA and Society Générale and the Chairmanship is on a rotational basis.

Few years back an employee of the Barclays bank, on 28 June 2012, manipulated the gold fixing process, leading to a payout, later identified. Barclay Bank, for which Financial Conduct Authority in 2014 fined Barclay bank Euro 25 million, reported the incident. This culminated into a new electronic price-discovery mechanism, scripted on 20th March 2015 to replace the long-established London Gold Fix. This means that the gold benchmark will be set via an electronic platform managed by the ICE Benchmark Administration and subsequently it declared, "IBA will operate a physically settled, electronic and tradable auction process. The price formation will be in dollars and prices will continue to be set twice daily at 10:30 and 15:00 (London time) in three currencies: USD, EUR and GBP. Within the process, aggregated gold bids and offers will be updated in real-time with the imbalance calculated and the price updated every 30 seconds until the buy and sell orders are matched. Participants, as well as sponsored clients, will be able to manage their orders in the auction in real time via their desktops." This essentially mean that no longer will the price be set through any private arrangement (conference calls twice a day) among just four members of London Gold Market Fixing Ltd. (at present, Bank of Nova Scotia-Scotia Mocatta, Barclays Bank PLC. HSBC Bank USA, and Society Générale SA). It brought more transparency to the market following the investigation into a number of global benchmarks set behind the closed doors, like the rigged Libor. More participants were involved into setting the benchmark price of gold comprising 11 entities that will provide the data for use of establishing the daily gold price and will make any collusion difficult to set the price.

The new gold price mechanism will involve a few Chinese banks who are LBMA members to participate in setting the gold prices and hence the Chinese clients will have a more direct influence on the international price of gold. The current eleven participants in the fixing are Barclays, the Bank of China, Bank of Communications, Goldman Sachs, HSBC Bank USA, JPMorgan Chase, Morgan Stanley, Society General, Standard Chartered, Scotia Mocatta (Scotia Bank), the Toronto-Dominion Bank, and UBS. The significance of this arrangement stems from the fact that the Chinese are found to be more bullish on gold. It is an open fact that the gold prices trade on an average at a higher price levels during the Asian trading hours than during the London and New York trading hours. This may provide a long-term support by ensuring larger transparency and stability and attract more value-oriented clients to the gold market.

☐ Price of gold and its making

The intrinsic value or proper worth of gold always remain constant. It is the price of gold in US dollars that changes and is said to be dollar price of gold. At the point the question that arises is when the dollar price of one ounce of gold goes up from $1100 to $ 1200, does gold price actually go up? It is the dollar value of gold that goes up. For this situation, the dollar has weakened and one would get less gold. The dollar price of gold is inverse of the dollar, a price hostile to the dollar. To get a global viewpoint on gold, one needs to examine the cross currency rates. Long time back, Indian Rupees was smashing against the dollar and gold sales were slowing down. That was not because Indian enthusiasm for gold was down. If the Indians were paying in rupees when gold was down in dollars, it was actually going up in rupees. Reasonably, there is a need to examine one's base currency and then think about gold in that space, not just in dollar space. In this manner, think gold in terms of quantity by weight and physical holding that matters, not the dollar price which keep changing because of market manipulations.

The investors often think that the laws of demand and supply drive prices of merchandise. From the point of view of global market for physical gold, what happens when there is a huge demand and no particular increase in supply? For what reason is this mismatch? To comprehend this we need to understand that there is a physical gold market and a paper gold market. The paper gold market involves various contracts. COMEX futures, Exchange traded funds (ETFs), gold swaps, gold leasing, forward contracts, and unallocated gold issued by LBMA banks. The derivatives, for example, futures, swap, ETF's leasing, forwards and unallocated gold forms the paper gold market, which can be multiple times the size of the physical market. This implies out of hundred individuals just a single entity can really get the physical gold. This functions well when there is a two-way market and contracts are rolled over until the point when individuals don't request physical delivery. The paper market is mobilized to certain depositories and storehouses in New York, London and some bank intermediaries that are members of LBMA. The floating supply reduces for leasing when the physical gold is moved from New York to Frankfurt. It reduces the gold accessible for short position in New York . This increased risk is covered for short position somewhere else in the physical market. In the physical market, the substantial purchasers of gold needs to get gold from the refineries as there are purchasers but few sellers and the overabundance at refineries run to about a month or two, such is the tightness of the physical supply side. Though China, Russia and Iran are amassing gold along with other national banks. China's account of gold accumulation isn't very transparent. China needs lots of gold and that too reasonably quickly to diversify its risk of huge dollar holdings in terms of export remittance and treasury holdings. The necessity is high to the point that even the biggest gold mining producers in the world won't have the capacity to satisfy and therefore it buys extra gold from the market secretly with the end goal of staying away from the price effect of transparent purchase. The international gold purchases by China, Russia, Iran, Turkey, Jordan reduces the available gold supply, and persistent demand appear to squeeze paper gold, and the inverted pyramid of paper gold contract is susceptible to collapse. The price suppression through paper gold market is being already made. At the point when the physical gold is in less supply, why the price isn't increasing? It is a result of massive sales in futures and immense short sales of unallocated gold that keep on holding the prices down. It is a phenomenon of struggle between physical and paper gold. At one hand are the central banks, bullion banks, hedge funds, and large buyers and on the opposite end are the individual investors.

Manipulation of gold and its price is not something new to the world. At the point when the dollar price of gold goes down all of a sudden without adequate relevant news, it can reasonably be found out that the market is under manipulation. In the past, similar manifestations were seen amid London gold pool 1960, or IMF or in US dumping gold in the late 1970's. More recently, IMF dumping 400 tons of gold in 2010 shows only price suppression. There are studies that capture these price manipulations. At the point when the objective of Federal central bank is to keep the price of gold in order, and not repeat like 2011, when the price climbed to around $1900 per ounce, at that point it must be manipulated from going further up. If the prices go down because of deflation, and as a central bank if it looks for weak gold price, it is in order with its expectation and no manipulation is required at that point.

For suppression of dollar price of gold, the most profound direct proven procedure is dumping of the physical gold that were done during London gold pool 1960, when members of Bretton Woods system, for example, Germany, UK, USA, dumped gold on the London bullion market to suppress the price of gold. There were similarly such endeavors made during the 1970s even after President Nixon moved dollar out of gold standards. Gold started with $35 and in the wake of shunning the gold standard, it went up to $45 per ounce and by 1980, it hit $800 per ounce. Amid this course of increase in gold price, USA attempted covertly to stifle the gold price with gold sales. From 1974 to 1980, USA sold around 1000 tons, made IMF sale 700 tons bringing about dumping of 1700 tons, which is about 5percent of central bank holding. Nonetheless, this did not work and thus USA surrendered resulting into the price settling to a stable value on its own. In 1999, UK dumped 66 percent of its gold amid Chancellor Gordon Brown's regime (and that too at the least price of past couple of decades). Switzerland was a gold seller in 2000s. At the point when the physical gold interventions were not working again then the paper gold manipulation began.

The most straightforward approach to paper manipulation is through Comex futures. At the point when a large sell order is placed short time before the end of session, this frightens the purchaser's market into bringing down their bid price and the lower price is transmitted to the world as the price of gold, discouraging investors and market sentiments. The price decline drives the hedge funds into dumping more gold as they hit 'stop loss' limits on their positions. A momentum is built up where selling generates selling and the price goes further down for no specific reason. It is how somebody might have preferred it that way. Finally, a bottom is established and purchasers step in but by then the damage is already done. Futures have huge amount of leverage in the proportion 20:1 and maybe more. Despite knowing the presence of brokers on the floor and also of the clearing agents, yet the market is non transparent as it is hard to know who the players are whether the purchasers, sellers or the ultimate customers that lends secrecy but the brokers usually know it. Paper manipulation is additionally done through Exchange traded fund (ETF) like GLD, which however is complicated. These ETFs are share of stocks, which is in a trust, which takes the market actors money, buy gold and puts in a vault. In the event that the price isn't enjoyed by the actor, the actor can sell the shares. It is additionally possible to have physical gold trading one way and ETF shares the other way making a 'spread ' or arbitrage between the two prices that exist from time to time. If the large bank, who is an authorized members in GLD, looks for arbitrage, sees the physical gold price trade at a higher price than normal shares (the shares that are linked to certain amount of gold), the bank sells the physical gold and at the same time buy the shares from someone in the market. The bank takes the shares to the trustees and cashes them in to get physical gold. The bank delivers the physical gold to cover the physical shortage and keeps the difference, a risk free arbitrage. This movement removes the gold from the warehouse and the floating supply decreases, which actually would have otherwise been available for trading to support the paper gold. This gold, when it goes to China or Loomis vault in Switzerland, is not a part of the floating supply any more, though still a part of the total supply. This dynamics progressively pushed the paper gold to rest on less and less physical gold, and that the available gold volume gets smaller as the Chinese, Russians, Iranians, Turkey accumulates gold.

The Hedge funds are presently prominent players in the gold market, which was not the case before. On one side were the small holders comfortable with gold coins or bars under possession while on the other side were the biggest holders, sovereign wealth funds and central banks. In the middle there were no institutions much involved in any case. Hedge funds have filled the middle ground of gold investors between retail and sovereign. To the hedge funds gold is another tradable commodity simply like coffee, sugar, corn, Treasury bonds and others. They use 'stop loss' limits when they set up trading positions on which they put a maximum amount willing to lose before they get out. When the limit is achieved, they naturally get out regardless of the long-term view of the metal. As such, they have a transient view of trading. At the point when a hedge fund needs to manipulate the gold market from the short side, it places a large sell order, drive the gold down a certain amount, and once it achieves that amount, these stops are activated at the funds that are long on gold. When the other Hedge fund reaches 'stop loss' limit it again sells that push the price further down. The Hedge funds does likewise in this way picking up momentum for all others to sell one by one. Toward the end, obviously, the price can work its way higher again when more funds get gold and after that the short side manipulators come enthusiastically for repeat performance. Without government regulation of hostile manipulation rules, these games will keep on occurring, until the point when a fundamental development drives the price to a higher path.

Gold leasing and unallocated forwards are methods of manipulating the price. At the point when large gold buyers need to purchase physical gold from major banks or merchants, they put an order at market price. The bank will get currency in lieu of a written contract in standard form wherein it will peruse to claim gold on 'unallocated' basis, which means there are no assigned bars, serial number registered against the owner's name. This enables the bank to sell the same gold many times over to numerous purchasers. This is like fractional reserve banking where banks appear to have as much cash as they have deposits and henceforth banks are found leveraged under the protection of the lender of final resort that is central bank. Banks sell more gold than they possess and if each holder of unallocated gold show up at once, there would not be adequate gold around. In view of security risks, storage costs, transportation and insurance costs, the holders are happy to leave it with the bank. What the holders probably would not understand is that the banks don't have it either. It is relevant to state here that central banks can lease gold to one of the LBMA banks, which includes HSBC, Citi, and JPMorgan Chase and is done through an intermediary called BIS Historically, BIS is an essential institution that manipulates gold markets for sale of gold between central bank and commercial banks. BIS can take lease of the gold from Federal Reserve and rent it out to any commercial banks that are LBMA members. The commercial bank will have title to a portion of the gold and will thus pitch tenfold of the amount to make a market place on unallocated basis. Hence, a favorable position is made out of the paper title through lease agreement.

Presently we realize that LBMA banks enthusiasm for manipulation is for making arbitrage and earn profits while the Hedge funds are in it for momentum profit. However, there are various players in the world who have political and policy interest and along these lines undertake to suppress price of gold. There are many who might assume that Federal reserve need to show strong dollar and consequently smother gold price though USA needs inflation for growth for which weak dollar should be the correct intention. Less expensive dollar prices imports more, which helps inflation targets, being net importer and when import prices increase, the inflation sustains through the supply chain in USA. Again, a weak dollar implies higher dollar price for gold. It is not that Fed would get weak dollar or strong dollar at whatever point it needs. There are factors that would not permit such wish. There are opposing forces, for example, deflationary tendencies from debts, socioeconomics, technology, deleveraging. The other force is that all nations need weak currency for competing exports. Striking back is not a reasonable choice that produces currency wars while the two currencies cannot devalue against one another at the same time. At times inspite of USA's economic policy in adverse, it needs to keep up dollar strong with the goal that other nation gets low interest to size up own economy.

☐ Position of Gold in Indian Economy

It is figured out that the aggregate gold reserve assessed on the books of Central Banks is around 35000 tons and that holding of RBI is a modest 558 tons. The Government of India has in possession some gold essentially out of confiscation of smuggled gold and some purchase made from International Institutions. RBI is not a buyer or a seller of gold reserve, unlike numerous other developing countries in Asia. A part of the gold was utilized by RBI in raising foreign currency resources amid Balance of

Payment emergency in 1990's. These overseas gold holdings are used as a major aspect of Reserve Management to yield a return.

The use of gold as a financial product is almost non-existent in India. To a restricted degree it is used in issuing 'Gold Bond' by the government which at times is combined with tax amnesty. The Commercial Banks however accept gold as security, but no debt advance is allowed for purchase of gold by the customers for non-productive use. India is known to have a lot of gold, around 22000 tons, accumulated over hundreds of years of trading and not out of its own production in the nation. The demand originates, according to available indication, from 80 percent of its use in jewellery fabrication (over 22 carats purity) to take care of the domestic demand, 15 percent for investment demand and rest for some industrial use. The demand for societal use is established in religious, ceremonial, preferred form of wealth for women, and a hedge against inflation, which is hard to prioritize, and is seen in combination. There is motivation to believe that a part of investment for gold assets is out of the untaxed money. The yearly consumption of gold, which was estimated at 65 tons in 1982, has increased in excess of 750 tons in 2017. With the economic growth and awareness, the demand in urban areas is probably going to diminish whereas it is probably going to increase with the thriving prosperity of the rural areas. Hence, there is no doubt demand will continue to grow in future. The domestic production is almost insignificant. The supply from manufactured gold scraps every year does not have any significant effect in the rising demand. Therefore, demand must be met from acquirement outside of the country. Notwithstanding, the official restriction on gold import for household use until 1990, the rising demand was met by unlawful imports. Amid 1968 to 1995, smuggled gold into

India varied from 10-217 tons with the special case of 1980 when 9.0 tons were exported to exploit rising gold prices in the global market. In the nineties, circumstance changed radically as the extent of pirated gold in India's aggregate supply went down considerably.

The strong demand for gold in contrast to restrictive policy measures is reflected in the more expensive rates of gold in the domestic market at the available exchange rate. The average spread between Mumbai and London market price from 1977-96 was in the positive, with the exception of 1980-81, when the worldwide gold prices increased during the oil crisis together with nonstop weakening of dollar. The flight of dollar resources into gold, added to the exception phase thereby accelerating inflationary trends globally. Without open market import, the domestic gold prices with respect to international prices appear to be governed by two variables. First, is the spread between official and market exchange rate of rupee and second is the combination of customs duty, transport and storage costs, risk premium and so on. Gold imports through official channels were assessed to have expanded from $1.25 billion in 1992 to $3.4 billion in 1995 while that of smuggled gold was in the range of $1.2-$1.7 billion. The gold import has risen second to oil in terms of significance in foreign trade. The management of demand and supply of gold has important policy implication for fiscal approach and exchange rate management and of late use and mobilization of gold as financial instrument has picked up consideration.

Since independence, the gold control policy rotated around five primary goals, to wean individuals away from gold, to regulate supply of gold, reduce smuggling, to decrease demand for gold, lastly to lessen domestic price for gold. It is interesting to peep into the policy measures since our independence. Bullion import and exports were prohibited under Foreign Exchange Regulation Act 1947. The official gold stocks of RBI were revalued. The proportional reserve system was substituted by minimum reserve system with the end goal of currency issue. A noteworthy effort started in November 1962 to mobilize vast gold reserve in the nation. This was with an issue of 15 years Gold Bond at 6.5% interest. Those bonds were issued in return for gold, gold coins, gold ornaments and the subscription of these bonds oversaw 16.30 tons. The issue of Gold bond was combined with urging public to abstain from purchasing gold and surrender their gold possessions to government. RBI approached banks to call for loans made against gold. Forward trading in gold was restricted in 1962. The diversion of saving into bullion market was controlled by declaration of Gold control Rules in January 1963. The Rules restricted manufacturing of gold jewellery of more than 14-carat purity. Individual gold holding had to be announced. Refineries were denied from manufacturing gold of more than 14 carats purity. By 1964, control over internal trade was completely established. There was a second endeavor to collect gold in 1965, when another series of Gold Bond at 7% was issued. Individuals who had unaccounted money were offered chance to convert into these bonds. The amount raised was just 6.1 tons. Further, a third series gold bonds assigned as National Defense Gold Bonds 1980 was issued, unlike earlier issues which were repayable in Rupees wherein the value of gold was determined in international prices. These bonds were redeemable in gold of standard purity at maturity and the amount raised was 13.7 tons.

The Gold control stayed in force until November 1966, when the guidelines were altered, lifting the prohibition on manufacture of jewellery of more than 14 carats purity. The revision set ceiling on individual holdings and extended control over refineries and merchants. In

September 1968, Gold Control Act was set up on permanent statutory basis with minor changes in successive years while the structure of control remained same. The voluntary disclosure of Income and Wealth Amended Ordinance 1975 conceded immunity from confiscation, penalty and prosecution to all disclosures of wealth and income as gold within a stipulated time. There was a major shift in government's approach in 1978-79 budgets. It unequivocally opposed smuggling activity emerging out of the difference in gold prices in domestic market from international. The government undertook gold auctions, considered as anti-inflationary measure, for fund-raising to finance budget deficit, which was around Rs. 1050 crores. It was thought to contain smuggling to some degree. The RBI worked as government operator in the business operation, met with serious criticism, and was later pulled back in October 1978.

The economic liberation acquired significant changes in regulation overseeing purchase and ownership of gold. Prior to 1991, gold allowed to be held as jewellery. This was canceled and from that point, holding gold bars and coins were allowed. The NRI baggage rule was qualified for bringing 5.0kgs of gold every 6 months by paying a nominal duty of Rs. 220 per 10 gms. Import of plain gold was permitted on Special Imprest license available to be purchased in the domestic market. The SIL scheme enabled a category of exporters to send back their overseas earnings by bringing in merchandise, which was previously restricted including gold bullion. The scheme in this manner was relaxed to permit import of gold jewellery and coins likewise. The government of Maharashtra unexpectedly disavowed the new tax of 2 percent presented earlier on value of processed gold. Further, a civic entry tax in Mumbai was reduced from 2 percent to 0.5 percent on April 1st 1996.

Notwithstanding, measures were debated at RBI for reduction of gold demand and its import into India and a few recommendations offered in 1978 to modify the consumption outlook to reduce demand for gold. Some of them were fixation of quantitative ceiling on holdings per family/individual, reduction of gold content in jewellery up to 14 carats, creating of alternative assets with attractive yield, for example, presentation of gold bond scheme/securities, imposition of tax on the jewellery component of wealth at higher rate, administrative measures for tax avoidance surpassing limits. These were considered in light of the five choices for import of gold as a practical socio- economic policy measure, import on a limited scale to meet specific purpose, if all else fails, as necessary evil and above all no import of gold. Similarly, the observations and discussions made on the level of gold prices were few. For larger part of the general population gold prices did not make a difference by any appreciably noticeable stretch. National economy got affected as they generate unofficial income, give a way to holding ill-conceived wealth and increase propensity to take part in illegal activity that help smuggled imports and unaccounted use of resources for payments abroad. Furthermore, had the price of gold taken off, it would have given safe means for holding gains, as well as makes such holding profoundly profitable. Gold was not to be viewed as an essential consumption by the poor and thus no reason for reducing the price of gold was felt. Some non-partisan views were presented to seek gold policy. The price of gold ought not involve government concern, as it doesn't enter the cost of living of the industrial and agriculture workers of India. Further, there was doubt about the system of auction that does not reduce smuggling or the price.

In 1978, a committee under the chairmanship of Dr. I.G. Patel, then Governor of RBI, was constituted to formulate a Gold policy. It was tasked to consider past policies and recommend to government some measures, for example, reintroduction of 18 carat or 14 carat jewellery by stages, and the procedure was required to be regulated in a way not to have any unfavorable impacts on small goldsmiths and artisans. The banking system should devise an effective scheme to give financial assistance to goldsmith at concessional rate of interest and a limit on individual holding of jewellery be confined to 2.0 Kgs and for family 4.0 Kgs. All things considered, because of strain in balance of payment around then, the report did not find adequate support favoring import of gold or for gold auction. RBI, however, was in support as it could accumulate gold to add to the official reserve as opposed to exports. Issuing gold bonds was not favored since it would basically amount to indexing the value of savings of the individuals who need gold as a hedge against inflation when compared to savers who were ready to hold other financial assets. A higher sales tax on jewellery was preferred with the end goal that it may go about as disincentive to wealth tax. In 1986, a Working group was established under the Chairmanship of Dr. C. Rangarajan to review Gold policy having reference explicit to import of gold, separate treatment of import of gold by returning NRI, bringing gold as personal baggage and non-utility of Gold control act as anti-smuggling measures. The perceptions offered were import of gold against free foreign exchange could not be allowed yet observed legitimacy in a scheme to pull in NRI funds on non-repatriation basis through 7 years deposits, denominated in foreign currency. The proposition to enable returning Indians to bring primary gold as part of baggage allowance may lead to large substitution of normal foreign exchange flows, aside from unmanageable enforcement, and raising the ceiling on value of gold jewellery imported under the transfer of residence rules and customs baggage rules. The government acted upon greater part of these proposals.

The discourse paper of RBI in 1992 perceived the significance of Gold in a changed situation underscoring its bearing on external debt. Thinking about the dynamics of demand and supply, an institutional mechanism of 'Gold Management Corporation' (GMC) was proposed. The GMC guided by the Gold Policy Board was to be developed into a mechanism that can develop and assess the required schemes for gold mobilization and accordingly its use in case of external imperatives. The policy towards gold import was to be founded on adequacy and effectiveness of gold mobilization and its use. Liberal import policy could be considered when the imported gold could be mobilized by way of channelizing it to RBI for reserve management. At last the recommendation was to induce the households to treat gold at par with other financial assets. In 1992, a proposition actively considered was to build up a Gold Bank with the objective of mobilizing domestic non-official gold holdings channelize them into a centralized pool over a period of time and to deploy them in a productive way in light of a legitimate concern for development and improvement of the nation. This proposition was not accepted and Gold Bond of 1993 was launched, which in aggregate collected 41 tons. Simultaneously, a committee within RBI made a few suggestions for Integrated national gold policy covering trading, import, jewellery exports, investment, refining and so forth despite the fact that rules exist in subsectors. Import policy for gold and silver to be further liberalized to stop smuggling and hawala activities. Select bullion associations in the country or some canalizing agency like SBI, MMTC might be permitted to import subject to prescribed ceiling. It felt the need to regulate country's

61

bullion market and introduce uniform trading practices everywhere throughout the country in view of high turnover in bullion trade and country's capability to become Centre for bullion trading. It promoted standardization of market practices that would lead to transparency in dealings, investor protection and market proficiency for wholesale trading in bullion. It was desirable to present forward trading in gold as a price hedging mechanism after further liberalization of gold import. Institutional arrangements to be made for regulation and standardization of bullion trade practices and for coordination with other agencies for which a separate statutory body called 'Gold Management Board' might be set up with statutory powers to monitor wholesale bullion operation and provide focus to the trade. The Board required finding a way to overhaul the standard and quality of refineries in the nation. Hallmarking of jewellery introduced in the country as a measure of consumer protection. Conceding of permission to the commercial banks in bullion trading to be deferred until the point that the import of gold is all the more freely allowed. The future schemes of mobilization of gold in the country left with agencies like mutual funds, which have more flexibility in operation. The mobilized gold might be offered to the jewelers to meet their inventory needs and to make the plan feasible. Instruments connected to gold price might be made available in the market to wean public away from physical gold. The above perceptions on gold policy liberalization met with some criticisms. India, being the biggest consumer of gold in the world, the aggregate quantity of gold imported legitimately in general has risen sharply. This deplete was on reserve. The liberalized policy of NRI route and SIL route had nil impact on smuggling. The purported NRI route was supported by ' hawala' market and expert NRI couriers were used to import gold through this route crushing its objective. The gold through this course, largely remain untraced inside India, as it is not traded in legal channel. In addition, late increment in gold smuggling is inferable from increased narcotics trade and any adjustment in policy tightening or loosening would be of little use. The main problem of 'hawala ' market finance is inefficiency in the staggering cost of bank services in dealing with NRI remittances from the Gulf region. The issue is not generally in export under-invoicing and import over-invoicing as a great part of the gold smuggling activity is Gulf focused and not in other major markets. There were different perspectives on offer also. Hawala margins have come down and there is increase in gold demand reflects genuine demand for gold jewellery, that calls for further liberalization of gold imports and improved market efficiency. As vast imports have not unfavorably influenced BOP or exchange rate and actually have given revenue to governments and incentives to exporters. Further liberalization would reduce transaction costs and the role of unsocial elements. There can be fiscal gains because of import and export taxes. Liberalization should be aligned with transparent regulatory mechanism as the central bank and the public institutions take monopoly in import of gold. While propelling a plan for urging general society to utilize gold as a monetary resource the RBI and Government can utilize their very own gold stock all the more productively and earn income. Institutional development to mobilize gold and allow their use as financial asset is important . Recognizing the need of forward trading in the age of liberalization is an important consideration.

With the purpose of management of Gold Reserve, the central banks of non-mining countries who have moderate gold possessions look to add value to discharge cost by utilizing a part or entire of their holding in the spot, forward or swap and lease markets. RBI had a modest holding of around 595.0 tons, one of the largest holdings among developing countries earlier. Traditionally, India held gold as an idle asset and now and again, these assets were utilized in the critical time of foreign exchange crisis as in 1991, which showed to the world that gold held in central banks lend support to the forex reserve of the nation. A part of the gold holdings of around 15 percent is located in offshore banks for short-term interest bearing deposits according to the provision of RBI Act. Locating gold at the offshore Centres involve cost yet for purpose of flexibility can be used to raise resources against gold which could be cost effective. It might not trade off the ownership and possession over stock. Indeed, even the Rangarajan Committee communicated the benefit of locating one-fourth of gold holding of RBI at offshore Centre that it could be used in the midst of need.

With the profound development of the financial sector and markets, it is conceivable that interest for physical gold, as a form of insurance cum investment would reduce. The availability of financial instrument in the nonfarm sector could help prepare mobilization of idle gold with family units. However, it is not appropriate to regard gold jewellery as idle asset as it is additionally used consumer durable. With the end goal to reduce hoarding demand, restriction on forward trading must be lifted to bring the idle gold into market pool. Necessary framework should be contrived for regulating the import, trading and market making in gold and related items for import liberalization. Again, the development of financial market in gold depends upon capital account convertibility. In spite of the fact that, banks can purchase sale and deal in bullion legally, yet gold control being in force until 1990 and FERA provisions, impose capital controls that enter the path of financial products denominated in gold.

Given that RBI and Government of India could assume a role in building up the gold market, except if the general stance on gold policy is positive, there remains a position of the gold policy in waiting.

☐ The Jewellery Heritage that makes India proud

Tradition of adorning oneself with jewellery is 5000 years old in India. Indian women and jewellery have always formed a great combination. There is jewellery for almost all the body parts, including neck, ear, nose, arms, ankles, fingers, waist, hair parting, etc. In India, jewellery is designed to match with the attire. The theme of its design as well as the colour of the jewellery is taken into consideration while adoring. To make jewellery more attractive, it is mounted by diamonds and various types of gems. Traditionally, Indian jewellery has been made of heavy and voluminous gold pieces, but recently jewellery made of silver, platinum and other metals has become quite popular among people. The popularity of jewellery made out of stone, encrusted on metal, has grown more recently. The different kinds of jewellery in India are briefly outlined.

Antique Jewellery is the jewellery which is not in mainstream production and its mode of production is no longer popular is known by the name of 'Antique Jewellery.' This jewellery has dull and rough look, combined with an old world charm, and this serves as the major USP of such jewellery.

Bead jewellery is an art in India and is five thousand year old that dates back to the time of Indus Valley Civilization. People of that civilization used to make beads out of gold, silver, copper, clay, ivory and even wood.

Bridal jewellery in India has great tradition and comprised of wedding jewellery. Made of superior metals and excellent quality, jewellery accentuates the beauty of bride in multiples. Though these days silver and platinum jewellery is gaining popularity, gold jewellery still holds the most popularity among Indians.

Custom Jewellery is personalized jewellery, which a customer orders and get produced according to her interest and fancy. This happens particularly in cases where readymade jewellery does not match the taste of the person. Custom jewellery gives total freedom to customer about the specifics of the jewellery.

Fashion jewellery is called costume jewellery, primarily for the reason that it is not made of precious metals and stones. Lighter and cheaper material are used. Fashion jewellery is highly trend-conscious and keeps on changing as per changing needs.

Filigree Jewellery work is done originally on silver and involves lots of precision and technicality, added with great amount of patience and an eye for minute details. Historically, filigree work was quite popular in countries like Egypt, Italy, and Spain. India's history of filigree work goes back to early centuries and has gained prominence in the gold jewellery as well.

Gold Jewellery prominently features Gold as a metal that lures many and talking about jewellery manufacturing in India is as good as talking about handmade jewellery in India. A major chunk of the jewellery in the country is made by independent artisans and artisans. Traditionally, a significant part of jewellery manufacturing has been handmade jewellery though machine made gold jewellery is found to gain popularity in the mainstream and part of the production process is in use as tools for making handmade jewellery.

Ivory Jewellery, historically, is made from the tusk of an elephant is called ivory jewellery. Importance of ivory jewellery can be guessed from the fact that in Gujarat, the bride receives an ivory bangle from her family just before marriage as jewellery. It is not much in vogue these days because of animal protection acts.

Jadau Jewellery forms one of the major examples of high skilled artisanship that was brought into India by the Mughals. Jadau jewellery is called engraved jewellery.

Kundan Jewellery came to India during the Mughal period and this art of kundan work reached Rajasthan from Delhi.

Lac Jewellery, known as lacquer jewellery, originated in Rajasthan and has gained considerable popularity in India today. Lac jewellery is available in versatile designs. Among the various items in lac jewellery, the bangles need a special mention.

Meenakari jewellery is another art form in which precious stones are set and then enameled with gold.

Navratna Jewellery, as the name suggests that nine auspicious stones are used in a single ornament. In India, Navratna jewellery has been given major importance, for its astrological significance and its innate charm.

Pachchikam jewellery originated in Kutch ,Gujarat , centuries ago which again has become popular.

In the world of fashion and design, old trends tend to come back repeatedly, though with slight changes. Pachchikam jewellery making craft is one of the examples of jewellery that has come back once again.

Silver Jewellery along with gold jewellery, is quite popular amongst Indian women. Ornaments made of silver, such as rings, bracelets, chains, necklaces, nose rings, earrings, toe rings, heavy kadas, and armlets, form integral part of Indian jewellery.

Stone Jewellery called studded jewellery with gems is quite popular among Indians. For reasons ranging from spiritual to aesthetic to health, gemstone jewellery has become the part of life of Indian women and men both. These stone jewelleries are worn according to the individual's astrological chart and ruling of planet.

Temple Jewellery is nothing but another form of Indian jewellery art, which at times is divided into three kinds - temple jewellery, spiritual jewellery and bridal jewellery. Temple jewellery of India initially used to be described as the jewellery used to adorn the idols of Gods and Goddesses. The statues in India were ornamented with chunky necklaces.

Tribal Jewellery in India is quite rich. Each tribe has kept its unique style of jewellery intact even now. The original format of jewellery design has been preserved by ethnic tribal. Jewellery that is made of bone, wood, clay, shells and crude metal, by tribal's, is attractive, but holds a distinct rustic charm.

The jewellery of India has played a significant role over the years in enhancing the beauty of the various classical performing dance forms like Kuchipudi, Kathak or Bharatnatyam, which are popular in India, by embellishing them with exquisite jewellery covering almost every part of the body. Even to this modern day, the demand for traditional Indian handmade jewellery has maintained its charm, which lies in the intricate designs by the craftsmen.

☐ India's approach to Export Policy

After independence in 1947, India's economic and trade policy primarily focused on self-reliance and less dependence on foreign trade as a source of revenue and income. The union government adopted the policy of import substitution and industrialization and developed a system of price controls and quantitative restriction. This led to an era of expansionary fiscal and monetary measures as late as 1980s that enabled growth to rise to 5.8 percent complemented by minimal current account deficit. Over time, mounting deficit with high inflation of around 13.5 percent coupled with the Gulf war in 1991 pushed Indian economy to balance of payment crisis. Having little option, Indian economy had to open its door to foreign participation for the first time through the process of liberalization that comprised policy reforms to improve efficiency and competitiveness of Indian industries. This enabled Indian exports into an engine of growth for the economy and the society that contributed to countries much required foreign exchange to national income. The outcome compelled the policy makers to recognize the growing importance of domestic and international policies that affect export performance of its products.

The Export Import Policy (EXIM Policy) that was announced under Foreign Trade Development and Regulation Act 1992, reflected the extent of liberalization and regulation that essentially addressed export promotion. This policy was announced for a period of Five years and annually it was reviewed based on broad frame of five years. In 1992, the features outlined in the EXIM policy were elimination of licensing, quantitative restrictions with other regulatory and discretionary controls. The Union Commerce Ministry announces the FTP every five years and is updated and modified annually with new schemes responding to global economic changes and practices to be competitive in international environment of exportable product. These considerations determine the export policy and strategy of the government passed on to the exporters and importers of goods through the various institutions of the country. In the age of globalization where all the countries are integrated to facilitate the flow of trade and commerce conducted under the supervision of the sovereign global institution of the likes of UN, WTO, ITC, UNCTAD, IMF,OECD to name a few, and each countries are vying for their fair share of trade and surpluses of commercial goods. The objective of determining the policy and strategy of India laid in facilitating sustained growth in exports and increase of market share of products that allow countries to access essential raw materials, components and intermediates, capital goods, consumables required for increased production and services. The other objective was to increase efficiency, enhance technological capability of Indian agriculture, industry and services, so that the competitive strength could be improved while generating new employment opportunities, and encourage globally acceptable quality standards. The policy adopted was to offer consumers with quality products and services at internationally competitive prices and at the same instance creating a level playing field for the domestic products. It is naturally imperative to understand the progression of FTP's and recognize the policy implications that determine the growth in exports over a period of the Gems and Jewellery Industry under various five years foreign trade policy. The 60's era that saw the government of India introduce the Replenishment (REP) License that allowed an importer to import rough diamonds of 80 percent of value of exports. The custom duty levied was 45 percent on rough imports. The FTP simplified the procedures to export of diamond jewellery comprising 70 percent of Gems and Jewellery exports. Branded and partially processed jewellery was allowed for export. The customs duty of 45 percent on rough gems stones and semi-processed diamonds were abolished in the Union Budget 2003-04. To give impetus to exports, the government establish Special Economic Zones (SEZs) and offer special incentives to units, Nil import duty on inputs, ten years income tax holiday, net positive foreign exchange, import and export not permitted in absence of Kimberley process certificate (KPCS). The cut and polished diamonds, precious and semi precious stones (except roughs) were allowed to take outside SEZs for subcontracting. Gem and Jewellery units were allowed to receive plain gold /silver/platinum from Domestic Tariff Area (DTA) or from Export Oriented Units (EOUs) in exchange of equivalent content of the same material contained in the said jewellery after adjusting for permissible wastage or loss as per ruling FTP and its procedures. The DTA units or subcontractors were not entitled to export entitlements. A special focus on exports of Gems and Jewellery through Market Access Initiatives (MAI) was initiated in EXIM Policy 2002-07 that contained duty free imports after adjustment of Value addition norms.

In 2004-05 budgets, import duty on platinum was lowered to $5.03 per 10 grams. Instead of claiming reimbursement later, customs duty on rough colour gemstones were exempted. Semiprecious stones were exempted to promote studded jewellery and platinum jewellery. Import of Gold of 18 carat under replenishment was allowed provided it is accompanied by an Assay certificate specifying purity, weight, and alloy content. Foreign Direct Investment (FDI) in Gems and Jewellery sector was allowed in 2007 and import duty on polished diamonds abolished with the representation from the trade. The cutting and polishing of gem and jewellery was treated as manufacturing and earned exemption under section 10 A of Income Tax Act. To revive the economy in 2008, after the financial meltdown, a slew of measures were announced wherein pre-shipment and post-shipment Rupee export credit was increased from 180 days to 270 days. Interest subvention of 2 percent up to March 2009, extended to the sector up to minimum of 7 percent interest

71

per annum to make pre shipment and post-shipment credit attractive. Exporters were allowed to avail refunds of service tax on foreign agent's commission up to 10 percent of FOB (free on board) value of export and of output services while availing duty drawback scheme (DDS). Banks were required not to charge interest rate exceeding Benchmark Prime lending rate (BPLR) minus 4.5 percent on pre-shipment credit of 270 days and post shipment of 180 days on the outstanding amount for the period December 1,2008 to September 30,2009. The service tax on exports was exempted in the annual supplement of FTP 2004-09, announced on April 2007. The re-import of diamonds and jewellery in complete or partial lot on consignment basis was allowed. The duty-free import entitlement was allowed for tools, machinery and equipments. The categorization of One to Five Star export houses was re-classified to export houses and trading houses with change in export performances. Hallmarking was made mandatory and import of polished diamond made duty free to establish a global trading hub of gem and jewellery. In the budget of 2008-09, rough cubic zirconia was exempted of import duty, while cut and polished cubic zirconia and rough corals were reduced from 10 percent to 5 percent. Under benign assessment procedure, the net profit rate in diamond manufacturing and trading sector reduced from 8percent to 6 percent. In 2009, Surat was recognized as a town of export excellence, home to diamond units employing large number of workers. The authorized persons of EOU units were permitted to carry personal carriage of gold in primary form up to 10 kgs in a financial year, subject to RBI and Customs guidelines while import restrictions on worked corals were removed. The Foreign Trade Policy 2009-2014, permitted duty free Import entitlement of consumables of metals other than gold, platinum amount to 2 percent of FOB value of exports during preceding year, of commercial sample INR

3.0 lacs duty free reimport entitlement for rejected jewellery up to two percent of a FOB value of Exports. For certification and grading diamond import on consignment basis for re-export, the Gemological Institute of America (GIA) in India was permitted to be the authorized agency. Again, the value limit of personal carriage was raised to US dollar 5 million for participation in foreign exhibition and US dollar 1 million for carrying samples for export promotion to augment export performance. Re-import of unsold items in exhibition extended to 90 days. To make India International Diamond trading hub, establishment of diamond bourse was planned which materialized years later. Several other measures initiated to promote exports like 10 percent of FOB value of exports of preceding year allowed to be sold in DTA, subject to positive Net Foreign Exchange (NFE) and for plain gold Jewellery concessional rate of duty was made available to exporters of sale of gold from nominated agencies. Often measures are taken to discourage exporters to sell items of less value addition that have impacts on metal consumption in coins and bars. In 2009-10 the customs duty on serially numbered gold bars and coins were increased from INR 100 per 10 gram to 200 per 10 grams. For other forms it was made INR 500 per 10 grams. For Silver it was raised to INR 1000 per kilogram and all the increase was applicable for personal baggage as well. In 2010-11, for the purpose of polishing, customs duty on rhodium was reduced to 2 percent. On gold ores customs duty was reduced to a specific duty of INR 140 per 10 grams of gold content with exemption of additional duty and so was excise duty on refined gold of INR 280 per 10 grams and import of such items were allowed. The only occasion when policy intervention was required to curb gold import was when the current account deficit was on the rise wherein import duty was raised successively from 2 percent leading up to 10 percent followed in addition by 80:20 rule in 2013. Several other measures were introduced like gold monetization schemes, gold deposit schemes and gold based financial products. Nevertheless, the recent introduction of GST is much favourable to the Gems and Jewellery Industry that offers 3 percent levy on gold jewellery, silver jewellery and 0.25 percent on rough diamond. The government continuously encourages the establishment of Gems and Jewellery SEZs, parks, common facility Centres, development of clusters and extension of Pradhan Mantri Kaushal Kendra to more than 600 districts across the country. It will go a long way to create infrastructure that will have the potential to boost exports and related services to realize the dream of "Make in India" possible.

☐ Gold-a nuanced approach

It is only recently that Reserve Bank of India has obtained around 8.46 tons of gold to add on to its aggregate holding of 566.23 tons. Earlier to this the purchase was made from IMF in the year 2009 and this was accordingly the last purchase made. This attracts many viewpoints. Few consider it either as an investment made for the purpose of diversification of asset to cushion against worldwide market risks, which in turn is brewing with rising interest rate of US dollar while some are of the view that the central bank has created a buffer for reclamation of Gold Bond Scheme. In whatever way it may be viewed, it is quite evident that central bank still considers gold as a form of money that has value, unit of exchange, preserves wealth, and most importantly which never really went away. Gold has been ignored publicly, perhaps deliberately, being called often as a "barbarous relic", especially when authorities with power were unable to create debt, printing money out of thin air. Gold has obviously lost some sheen by the removal of gold standards, but again there exists no way to protect savings from confiscation through inflation. The boundaries pushed due to creation of debt money were so far and wide that in absence of any gold standards today, the real value of benchmark dollar as a currency has almost disappeared relative to gold. Whereas the central banks have to compulsively hold on to gold so as to hedge against risks, while suggesting its own citizens to move away from gold simultaneously. This creates a serious question as to who will trust the bankers?

India's love for gold originates from the gold jewellery consumption attached to women emotions, tradition, culture, weddings, rituals, festivals and household ceremonies. Undoubtedly the demand for gold will continue to rise even more because of the fact that the gold jewellery may appropriately be classified as a consumer durable like any other products in the category, and is not an idle asset. Apart from its role as a "status symbol" or a mean for showcasing of wealth, it bears a subjective value to its wearer. Considering the fact that individuals can use only one particular durable item at a time, will it not render most of human possessions stored in cupboards or garages as idle? For example, a person having more than one cars, cell phones, houses, apparels, watches, shoes, and sundry other costly entities may be regarded as surplus and idle in which money gets locked. What then is the definition of idleness? Introduction of gold futures on Indian Commodity Exchange has not deterred the appetite for physical holding of gold. Therefore, what makes gold idle, the much rehearsed litany?

Gold has always been found to be treated differently. Post independence, the gold control policy was drafted to regulate the gold supply, diminish the demand for gold, reduce price, reduce smuggling, yet people of India could not be moved away from gold. There were policy measures to discourage the import of gold, one such involving increase in its import tariffs. With a view to reduce reliance on imports and to meet the domestic demand for gold in physical form and to mobilize the idle gold, a policy was launched back in 2015, in the name of "Gold Monetization Scheme", a new version of the erstwhile Gold Deposit scheme of 1999 or Gold Metal Loan of 1990. In the current scheme, the depositors of gold were to be given a certificate specifying the amount and purity of the deposited gold. Once the investors agrees to do so and after the fire assay test is done by the Collection and Purity Test Centres (Certified by BIS), the customer subsequently submits this certificate to any designated branch of a bank to open a gold savings account, subject to Know Your Customer norms. Accordingly, the customer account would be credited by the bank with an amount equivalent to the quantity of standard gold of 995 fineness, and that would be based on the prevailing market price. Usually it is the bank who pays for the fire assay tests. In this scheme, the minimum amount of gold that could be deposited is 30 gms. in order to encourage the small depositors. The three categories under which GMS operate are namely short term deposits (1-3 yrs) with 1 year multiple rollout, medium term (5-7 yrs) and long term (12-15 yrs). The short term deposits are accepted by banks on their own account while the medium and long term are accepted by banks on behalf of the Government of India. The interest and principal on the short-term gold deposits would be denominated in volume that is gold in grams and the rate of interest would be decided by banks on prevailing market conditions and international lease rates. The medium and long term deposits and its interest rate would be denominated in Indian Rupees decided by the GOI in consultation with RBI. From available sources, public sector banks indicate to offer 0.50 percent interest for one year, 0.55 percent for two years and 0.60 percent for three years, while the government offers 2.25 percent in medium term and 2.50 percent in long term deposits. The schemes are attractive only to the tax payers as interest income from these deposits is exempt from tax. It is exempt from wealth tax and capital gain tax on appreciation in the price of gold. How will it be attractive to the small individual household savers? The policy does not draw much attention from the citizens as it does not address the emotional attachment of investors for the physical gold and does not have any reasonable improvement over the previous Gold Deposit Schemes. Moreover, appreciation in value of gold may not always happen. All of the above might speak of deficit trust in government schemes and individuals might choose physical gold as better alternatives.

The narrative that the gold collected from this scheme would be utilized as supply to jewellers and may act as a substitute for import were not bought by public. At the same time, the gold backed bond in paper was declared which could later be liquidated at the same price that might earn some success as an investment product for investors, but not to the jewellery consumers. The question that arises is-why the government wants public savings for its own end and what is the need to acquire physical gold for paper?

Gold is a typical element that preserves wealth in situations such as financial instability or downturn and goes about as safe haven that is without any risk unlike paper currency or fiat currency. Gold is known to be medium of exchange, store of value and regularly serving as a unit of exchange. It is realized that India has vast supplies of gold that are accumulations resulted from hundreds of years of trading and not a production of nations mines. The demand for gold is rooted in societal preference for a few reasons which is exceptionally hard to prioritize, like a favored form of wealth to women, religious, ceremonial and as a hedge to inflation, yet sensible to conclude its combined effect. Again, gold is not paper. These contentions justify that gold appeared not to have gone away. Had it been so worthless, why would USA hold on to 8000 tons, Euro zone to 10783 tons, Germany and IMF to 3000 tons each and for what reason would China procure 1000 tons yearly if they don't see gold equivalent of money and an ideal instrument of hedge?

Alternatively, the appeal of precious metals to criminals rests on the fact that it is used in AML/CFT for its high value , compactness, odourless, tradable in cash, and can be held without records as safe investment. Hence, it is an alternative currency to buy prohibited goods. This has compelled the authorities to track its role in cross border movements through myriads of FATF regulations and controls, that require multilateral interventions, which further requires in-depth understanding. The set standards for technical compliance and adequacy, ready with beneficial ownership and legal person ideas are eventually for tax reasons which are likely to increase after implementation worldwide. The compliance measure for the Precious metal and stones might increase the tax commitments and revenues covering the small tax payers presently out of the system. The money that was once printed at will by the central banks, will it be possible to recover from public through these tax mechanisms? Can the recovery unlock money tied in assets that comprises of non performing assets? Can the banks hope for additional liquidity from tax recoveries? Will there ever be opportunity for balance sheet normalization? What will happen this time in case of financial crisis ? Will the much practiced bail-out be a solution or a new instrument in the form of Bail-in be invoked? What ultimately is in store for the population? What will be the role of gold in the entire spectrum of events that have chances to unfold? These answers lie only in the future.

Another aspect that was gaining momentum in the last few years was the establishment of Shanghai Cooperation Organization and the BRICS bank whose purpose was kept abstracted from public. Countries that are trading in commodities outside of US Dollar, are engaged in bilateral trades for movement of goods using their own currencies. Are the currencies in use backed by gold? Why China, Russia, Turkey, Iran and to no less extent even India are looking for amassing gold? Why is there a shift in gold from west to east and what will happen to the drain of gold from European vaults and what impact will it have on their currencies? Are we moving towards a multi polar world? What made China and Russia to trade in their own currencies and what backs their currencies? Why China had to create Shanghai Gold Exchange and how is it being used in international trade? Why India should not have Gold exchange and what criterion is required to fulfill to become a fullfledged member of SCO and how much gold will be available to pledge for membership?

USA has been a consuming country and the largest importer of foreign goods worldwide. The Federal reserve banking system established in 1913 allowed USA to be the largest importer of goods as well as largest exporters of dollar currency throughout the world. It is tired of printing money to get the world economy out of recession and slow growth. In the process its own debt to GDP ratio substantially increased. Considering it wants to reduce budget deficit and also wants to export. Now, it looks to prioritize export, wants cheap dollar to compete. To get the dollar cheap or to devalue, first it has to get back the dollars residing in foreign countries. The only way to achieve it is to raise its own interest rates so that the dollar makes its flight back for higher gains. It cannot do so suddenly as the dollar is paired against major economy currencies which is globally integrated. In order to avoid a financial turmoil it has to step up the interest gradually. Once the dollar comes back it can then devalue. But the countries who hold dollars or dollar denominated securities will have to take positions. Right now, China holds more than $3.0 trillion from export surplus most of which are in US treasuries and it will never want its hard earned money to devalue. Since the weakness in dollar has become symptomatic, other countries might choose to come out of dollar bonds and dump treasuries. But China has to walk its way out stealthily. There has to be some kind of arrangement between the two largest export-import countries in the world. At one hand China has to hedge against its dollar exposure while on the other hand it has to create an alternative to trade outside of dollar between countries. What could possibly be the role of gold? Will it act as a bridge in the migration and is this why China has been buying gold from international market despite of its own production of 700 tons per annum? Or is it IMF which inducted Chinese Yuan making it the fifth currency in the IMF basket along with gold that lends support to the Special Drawing Rights, a form of money not owned by any country? Will SDR be used to stabilize the world financial system and is there a chance of benchmark currency reset? Are we already witnessing the dominant role of gold once again? Have we ever tried to understand how much the dollar currency has devalued since Bretton wood when one troy ounce cost $35 and what would be its price today assuming that the world wants to return on the gold standard again? Will it not be astronomically above our expectations? Though we cannot afford to cause another such Great Depression and hence SDR backed by gold could be a possible answer and it is the gold that has to play its stable role as money in transit.

CHAPTER 2

The Jewellery Matrix

☐ The Marketing Matrix of Jewellers

T

he jewellers adopts marketing methodologies depending on the specific markets they operate. Techniques applied for drawing in and influencing their clients rely on the marketing behavior of the jewellers engaged in the competition at the market they operate, taking into consideration in large measure the attitude of the customers. By analyzing the likings of the customers they end up recognizing their needs and accordingly design the jewellery. For doing so they may even go to the extent of customizing their jewellery design so as to acquire customer loyalty and further are open to provide after sales service which may include free repair, cleaning of jewellery and similar other services. For any business to prosper, marketing has a vital role. Similarly, here too various marketing tools like offer on making charges, gold harvesting, digital marketing, hallmarking etc are used. Irrespective of such alluring schemes, the concept of web based purchase isn't uncommon to a majority of population. Despite of the many advantages that the web purchase may provide, still there is a major group of people that appreciate purchasing with a feel of individual touch that inspires and fascinates them. With time and more awareness, customers search for more choices available these days while spending money, and in constant search of value proposition that fulfill their emotional needs. The jewellery retailers and actors working in a focused domain are influenced from traditional techniques to embrace most recent offerings of branded jewellery, exchange offers, financial facilities, transport facilities, lucky draws, festival sponsorships, unique offers, gifts, price discount, refreshments, individual attention and numerous different forms developing frequently.

Keeping in mind the golden rule of business which states "Customers are king" the motto of effective business is to comprehend the customer's need that includes creating techniques and studying the inspirational components in the purchase of jewellery. Components that inspire a customer in the formation of purchase decision is regularly studied by jewellers in terms of taste, purchasing powers, lifestyle, fashion orientation and comparative characteristics that tend to leave impression on potential future purchase. It is essential for the jewelers to understand the thoughts, desire, needs of all customers entering their fancy showroom and the level of satisfaction that they have at the time of leaving the showroom. Such understanding enables them to confront their customers confidently with an intention of persuading them for settling their purchase decision which ultimately help in achieving a superior business performance and proficiency. It is fundamental to comprehend the purchasing procedure of the customer, as they generally pursue a standard process in making purchase decisions, which allow retailers in focusing on advertisement and requisite marketing mix to tempt the customers to enter their shops for purchase. For achieving the above objective, skills needs to be acquired and such skills involves identifying various factors which may include recognizing whether it is for marriage, birthday or commemoration, mindful of whether male or female, whether genuine or casual, purchasing power or out of pressure to buy, the alluring schemes and offers or simply the relationship that determine the purchase of a customer from a specific shop.

All these investigation have led to the development of an array of systems related to the purchasing behavior and pattern that tend to depict and govern the purchasing decision of customers. A traditional jeweller always believes in public relations and commitment which can be viewed as effective tool in promoting and marketing his jewellery business. The customer base is developed through the means of awareness and keeping customer educated of the happenings in the business and in this manner updating of jewellery types according to customer requirements. Such marketing strategy includes ways to associate with the customer and their needs, which involves quite a bit of creative energy that can draw the attention of the customers. To gain the market share many jewelers are coming up with exciting schemes that could make the common man's dream of buying designer jewellery possible. It is a fact that India loves gold and just by using this concept jewellers or service providers are offering multiple facilities like credit finance to advance deals depending upon the credit score of people. This is achieved only because of the effort of these jewellers to tie-up with financial product companies to enable or provide the people with such installment facilities in urban areas. Not only is it all available for the urban people, but for rural areas multiple facilities such as replacing old jewellery for new ones, where the difference in amount can be paid in easy installments. Customers willing to buy in the present for payment later are pulled in to such methodologies that are found very viable The exchange offer is a common technique embraced to set up goodwill by the jeweller to expel slightest doubts in the mind of the customer about purity of gold jewellery. The exchange happens in terms of same purity that makes common belief and trust. Lucky draw strategy is another form to enhance sales wherein purchase far beyond certain amount of jewellery place the customer eligible to participate in a lucky draw with appealing proposition, for example, holiday package, cars, gold and so forth.

To build in loyalty and own shop brands, customers are often provided with transportation facility, an attractive option, as high value jewellery is viewed a risk in travel. Jewellers engage in supporting events, occasions, sports, trophies, for the purpose of promoting their brand through dynamic presence in social events. Another common promotion measure is to offer gifts like gold or silver coins for purchase over certain amount of the articles. Other schemes like offering discounts on M.R.P and refreshments for making a situation of relaxed purchase process, sometimes with a touch of personal attention by staffs that build up close personal relationship with the customers. Different measures and schemes adopted by jewellers to attract customers for enhanced sales performance is in constant state of development.

Another pattern fast gaining market in India is the sale of branded jewellery which is considered as the eventual fate of the industry and the growth of which is subject to acceptance of the customers, which again is reliant on awareness, knowledge and availability of the product. The selection of the media and in combinations offers space for information dissemination that is critical. Jewellery that was purchased, as investment choice on the foundation of value appreciation and as a part of security measure during stormy days, will most likely leave space for more consumption of branded jewellery as the potential Indian economic cycle improves in lieu of demographic advantage. A few investigations of McKinsey uncover that the branded jewellery will offer itself to compete some other white goods consumer products that please the customer in enhancing beauty as a part of attire and satisfy the desire associated with the product. The fragmented jewellery market and the scale of unethical practices generally ruled out branded jewelleries to prosper. Developing trust through educating customers of exploitative practices and changing the perception of jewellery purchase as a high value purchase can possibly change the mentality of customers from blind trust to informed trust. This technique whenever seeded in right viewpoint can lure and wean away customers from traditional stores. The development of product differentiation strategy in a high commodity-oriented condition, through offerings such as new designs, assume a significant role of pulling in customers. The accentuation on design is based on national character that a brand assumes; its nonexclusive design concept with some regional variation is fast advancing. This requires brand companies to establish a design team or outsource design for continuous development, meeting the changing tastes and demand, and is conceivable upon feedback and collection of information on customer's preference. Normally, control needs to assume a prevailing role in the whole set up. 'Tanishq' is a valid example that emphasizes on purity of gold, bolstered by advertisement campaign that underscores on purity aspects, progressively making differentiated products like light weight jewellery at reasonable price points, concentrating on urban and small towns where returns on investment are observed to be optimum. Another company perceived the need to move jewellery's from intensely guarded jewellery stores to dressing table by means of persuading lifestyle stores to include branded jewellery in their basket of products. It is no big surprise that the online jewellery sales are rapidly making up for the lost time with the experimental use of different metals like titanium, steel with different precious and semi-precious colour stones for regular use that offer impulse purchase. The product differentiation, unlike traditional jewellery, offers seasonal purchase offers that generates possibilities of buying throughout the year. This technique enables a few companies to fabricate products in consonance with high productivity, accomplish consistency and limit metal loss that counter the traditional jewellery making.

It should be clear by now the different strategies, motives, methodologies of the traditional jewellery manufacturers to protect and retain their customers. And not to forget the serious challenges that is expected to transpire from the so called "Branded Jewellery" segment.

☐ The future of manufacturing

"Change has always been a key to improvement" in every business. Similarly, over the time the jewellery industry has been evident to many dynamic changes and improvement in technology. The current flood of machine based manufacturing especially in computerized digital technologies, CAD/CAM and Rapid prototyping and manufacturing, which identify with the use of traditional technologies like lost wax or investment casting, powder metallurgy to name a few is gradually on the rise.

Improvement in the sphere of precious metal alloy technology has lead to upgraded manufacturing process superior in performance when worn by customers. Without a doubt, the computerized technologies will have a prominent impact and the present limit of traditional technologies like investment casting and powder production will push to look for new boundaries. It is an undeniable fact that the interest for machine made technologies will increase but at the same time the older technologies are expected to survive with renewed development. The enthusiasm towards efficient use of materials and yields will prompt decrease in cost, scale, design opportunities and customize designs, which will observe noticeable priority. There will be more demand for ethical and sustainable jewellery that are lightweight, strong, innovative designs, empowered by Rapid manufacturing technologies as in laser sintering or melting process, improvements in the use of blended colours, coating, alloying, to give another new design effects and improved performance to the wearer.

In the new frontiers, specialists like Dr. Christopher Conti and Johnson Matthew proposes in the outlook ahead that it isn't sufficient to just think about material, machine and procedures. However, the studying of components affecting the design trends and market forces have a bearing on the technical requirements and its advancement in new techniques. In the sphere of design and market rates the previous decade has witnessed increment in labour and manufacturing costs that has led to increase in mass produce. The low and moderately priced jewellery has moved to the eastern world like China, India, Thailand, for low cost labour. The quality of products steadily improved and opened up the local markets. Eastern markets got attracted towards the Western manufacturer's innovative design leadership of Italy and Europe. These trends have resulted in putting sufficient pressure on the Eastern manufacturers to reduce the cost through enhanced productivity and use of most recent machines or technologies and best practices. A "Lean Manufacturing" just-in- time approach has emerged, boosting value in the pipeline so as to keep up with the growing market share. Nevertheless, Far East has successfully grasped this change as early as possible and moved from craft based workshop of traditional goldsmiths to present day machine technologies, involving cutting edge processing plants.

The trend and inclination in Europe and the western world for white precious metal jewellery–silver, white gold, platinum, palladium, with rise in prices of metals, have put pressure on improvement of alloys and the assembly process with emphasis on lightweight jewellery. This gave rise to the prevalence of 'branded jewellery" with huge brands meeting the top of the line needs and design led sectors, where high margins have been achieved at ideal volumes. This has pushed the reason for 'customized jewellery', each piece with a design unique to the customer. The computer-based technologies have empowered such market patterns to life as new designs and products tends to get into the market faster. Given the backdrop, the customers of jewellery demonstrated more enthusiasm for ethical use of materials that is safe and has been made in socially responsible environment unlike the use of nickel in white gold that causes skin hypersensitivity.

☐ MSME schemes that languish for need of awareness

In India, the business environment is generally informal and the mindset of entrepreneurs is not programmed in a way to register their businesses in the beginning. It is known that the informal sector adds to nations GDP in large measure and provides maximum employment. The technocratic period that arrests job growth, has hurled difficulties to the agile hands of youth of India whose average age is expected to be 27yrs by 2020. Therefore, it is binding upon India to organize a superior business condition within the current situation of incentives and subsidies to encourage the youth to select business as a lifelong career choice. The greatest challenge starts with the familiarity of different schemes and plans available that are served through various Ministries at Union and State levels. Whenever offered under one umbrella may possibly energize the prospective entrepreneurs with little handholding that may bring about an increased productivity and efficiency in their ventures. Such information empowers small ventures to plan and compose business structure in terms of organization, cooperatives, partnership, proprietorship and such others to facilitate development, establishment, expansion, modernization, acquisition and mergers. Due to this the economic prospects increases alongside the upgraded knowledge of the scale of development, infrastructure, fiscal issues and export prospects.

There are different schemes that are set up for the Micro Small and Medium Enterprises (MSME) under the consideration of the government. Few of the plans are direct from government-recognized associations, councils, boards and other similar bodies for the immediate benefits of entrepreneurs. The schemes accessible extensively under SME division are under certain set of conditions available on MSME site (Forms and applications), that offers to give financial assistance on international cooperation, establishment of new institutions like Electronic Data Interchange (EDI), fortifying infrastructure for EDIs like deputation of MSME business delegates to different nations for the sake of technology infusion, up-gradation, Joint Ventures, international exhibition. It professes to give help to training institutions as capital grants, entrepreneur development program, skill development programs, marketing assistance support, organizing exhibitions abroad and participation in trade fairs, co-sponsoring exhibition, BSMs, marketing promotions, events and campaigns. Correspondingly, under Development Commissioner (DC-MSME), there are several other related schemes, for example, Credit Guarantee Schemes in which MSME and Small Industries Development Bank of India (SIDBI) jointly established a trust named Credit Guarantee Fund Trust in the name Credit Guarantee Fund Trust for Micro and Small Enterprises (CGTMSE) to actualize the plan. The Credit Linked Capital Subsidy Scheme for Technology up-gradation offers to induct state-of-the-art technology that enhances efficiency, quality and work environment for the units, including packaging, anti-pollution measures and energy conservation. Another related scheme for small-scale sector to improve competitive strength is on ISO 9000/ISO14001 Certification reimbursement, an incentive to neutralize the expenses on securing the technology to a certain degree. The Micro and Small Enterprise Cluster Development Program (MSE-CDP) is a related scheme that proposes to improve productivity, competitiveness, capacity building, and service providers, situated in close proximity that may offer the administration to economically reduce the cost of enterprise. The goal of cluster development is on technology, skill, quality improvements, access to the market and capital. Building of capacity through Self-Help groups, associations, consortia for common supportive action can create infrastructure in the new and existing industrial region or clusters, including formation of Common Facility Centres (CFC) like testing, training Centres, raw material depots, effluent treatment complimenting the production process. Assistance is provided for Diagnostic study, Soft Intervention, CFC, Infrastructure development or up-gradation under certain financial limits and conditions that include Hard Intervention and many others. There are other financial related plans for underserved states and pockets of the state under SIDBI. There is another MSME scheme related to Market Development Assistance (MDA) to MSME units to increase the participation of representatives belonging to participating units. A few different plans exist for MSME promotion that is The National Award scheme, National Manufacturing Competitiveness program, which contains ten other plans. This includes Design clinics, Marketing support, Barcode, Managerial development, Quality administration standards, awareness on Intellectual Property Rights (IPR), Lean Manufacturing Competitiveness scheme, Technology up gradation, Credit rating schemes, Bank credit facilitation scheme, Raw material scheme, Single point registration scheme, Info-mediary services, Market intelligence services, Bill discounting schemes and the likes. The schemes examined above might be benefited through Union government run offices and through offices of the State governments that are often aligned to the industrial policies adopted by the individual states in sectors that it normally excels and are invested for business development.

The vast majority of these schemes in jewellery sector calls for enlisting their units under Udyog Aadhar in which units may contact District Industries Centre (DIC) to look for help. To "Fund the unfunded" a flagship scheme "Pradhanmantri MUDRA (Micro Units Development and Reliance Agency Ltd) Yojana, has been propelled to bring the enterprises to the previous financial system for extending affordable credit. Micro and Small enterprises in the non-farm sector, occupied with manufacturing, trading and services requiring credit up to Rupees 10 lakhs are qualified to avail. The loan requirement is grouped into classifications like Shishu (up to 5 lakhs) Kishore (between 5 to 10 lakhs). Jewellerys units may benefit Credit Linked

Capital Subsidy for Technology Up grade (CLCSS) under National Manufacturing Competitiveness Program (NMCP) to look for 15 percent subsidy for additional investment up to Rupees 15 crore by inducting cutting edge or a close to cutting edge technology. (http://www.dcmsme.gov.in). The MSE Cluster Development Program (MSECDP) considers four noteworthy areas of support. Financial related help for conducting Diagnostic study on SME cluster of Rupees 2.50 lakhs, Soft intervention exercises for cluster units for technology, intervention, promotion of market and hand holding to cluster members are limited to Rupees 18.0 lakhs for competition in one and half years. The financial support offered for increase in productivity, capacity building at CFC, and effluent treatment plant et cetera is dependent upon Rupees 15.0 crore of project cost wherein 70 percent is a contribution by Government of India. Further, for the need of creating or upgrading the infrastructural facilities by virtue of power distribution network, telecommunication, water, drainage and pollution a limit of Rupees 10.0 crores of project cost in which 60 percent is a contribution from the Government of India. With the end goal to build manufacturing competitiveness, MSMEs may fall back on Lean Manufacturing (LM) techniques for which financial assistance exists for implementation purpose. The Consultant for LM technique who gives such service to the Special Purpose Vehicle (SPV) are paid their cost up to 80 percent from the government and remaining 20 percent from the beneficiary units which are subsequent to raising of bills for reimbursement and necessary applicable arrangements from NMIU, which in turn gets the fund from Ministry of MSME. The payment made by SPV to LM expert is in 5(Five) portions of 20 percentage for every milestone reached. The assistance for Barcode registration to MSME units is one time reimbursement of 75 percent. The remaining 75 percent of yearly recurring fee for initial three years paid to Geological Survey of India (GSI) by SMEs under NMCP is for the barcode use. The other plan available to the jewellery SMEs is the Marketing Assistance and Technology up gradation that looks to encourage developing domestic and overseas markets, setting up linkages through Vendor Development Program and organizing national and international seminars and workshops for spreading awareness and education. The scheme offers Rupees 2.50 lakhs for participation in International Trade Fair and rupees 30.0 thousands for domestic exhibition. (For more visit site http://www.dcmsme.gov.in). To organize exhibitions abroad or co-sponsoring of exhibition, BSM, campaigns, Marketing Assistance Initiative (MAI) is available with an overall ceiling of Rupees 30.0 lakhs per event in support and for all Latin American nations an extra Rupees of 10.0 lakhs is available for the event. Essentially, organization of domestic fair will involve components, for example, space rental including construction and fabrication charges, theme pavilion, printing material, advertisement, transportation, all according to a budget of Rupees 45.0 lakhs. The participation in exhibition of Rupees 15.0 lakhs is the corresponding limit of the budget. Financial assistance ranging from 25 percent to 95 percent of the airfare and space is available to entrepreneurs on the strength of the enterprise.

The promotional bodies that are responsible to attract the MSME beneficiaries through various awareness campaign measures are primarily the Directorate of MSME, State Industrial Development Corporations, MSME development institutes, SIDBI, GJEPC- India, GOI, Gem and Jewellery Trade Council of India and other Federations and Associations. Given the lack of awareness of these beautiful schemes on offer for the MSMEs and the department's lack of proclivity to reach out, did not accrue much benefits to the jewellery sector, both in terms of capital investment and employment generation. It has become imperative to project success stories in the finished jewellery segment that has benefited from the schemes, which may be symbolic for other MSME units to draw confidence and emulate.

☐ The concept of Lean manufacturing technique

The idea of Lean manufacturing techniques (LMT) was first found to be mentioned in a concept paper of Department of Industrial Policy and Planning (DIPP) and that it expects the MSMEs and SMEs to adopt for remarkable improvements in all segments of a manufacturing system. It has not escaped the attention of the Gem and Jewellery sector given the prospect of growth, its service in the time of stagnation in exports coupled with the possibility of transcending the domestic jewellery market into an organized structure. Industry offers managers and practitioners in recent time to make attempt to enhance productivity and eliminate wastes through LMT wherein the quality, cost, just in time delivery and continuous improvement have received more attention. Though many organization around the world have attempted to implement LMT to thrive in today's competitive global market, but lack of clear comprehension of its performance and measures have led to companies struggling to establish Lean manufacturing system.

The concept of lean manufacturing originated from Toyota a Japanese automaker, thriving for decades in global competition. Post WW2, to survive with minimum resources due to vast shortages of material, financial and human resources. Toyota production system was compelled to adopt waste reduction policy as a strategic goal to achieve. During adverse economic conditions,

Toyota sustained and prospered because of high efficiency and productivity. Taiichi Ohno, founder of TPS, published his experiences as former chief engineer for developing and improving processes at Toyota that led the theoretical foundation of the lean principles and management. The word Lean was first introduced by MIT professor to interpret Toyota's new production systems that does away with mass production as applied by Henry Ford. "Lean Production" was coined to be highly efficient production system that uses less of every resource to produce the same or even more amount of products ensuring competitive quality and cost. Over time "Lean" has assumed several views. Some consider it as a toolbox full of tools and techniques which when selected correctly can improve what is needed, while some consider it as a system where a company can achieve reduced costs with continuous improvement and customer satisfaction. Nowadays, "Lean" concept and related tool are expanded beyond the shop floor so as to implement in administrative work, supply chain and service sectors.

The Lean system of production is not implemented on isolated principles but an integrated system approach where people's knowledge is critical to sustainability. LPS is more than redesigning some production process where the focus is not on the methods, tools, change of layout, and process of production, rather on the critical factor that is people related than technology related, where understanding and integration of knowledge is regarded important. There exists strong interrelation between organizational structure and knowledge management in LPS, because knowledge is transferred between different roles in the organization. The common barriers identified that require adaptation are the leadership, organizational culture, planning, organization structure, and LPS knowledge.

Therefore, transition to LPS is challenging particularly because of the enterprise's principles, methods and tools changes that affects each employees in every position. The implementation of LPS starts with centrally controlled tasks as the first phase of the four phases, decentralized with the progress of other phases of implementation. The first phase comprises of the awareness of management that an LPS would contribute to its long-term sustainable development which is then followed by Lean assessment and strategic planning wherein the whole organization with its stakeholders, strategic objectives, business process and methods are analyzed. In the conceptual design of LPS, a central steering committee is installed to monitor and control the implementation process and thereby evolving the master planning of LPS implementation. The second phase is decentralized that starts with organizational changes regarding LPS implementation, resulting in central organizational structure and the local structure is then put in place with the detailed planning of implementation. The third phase is completely decentralized and takes place in the department of organization or enterprise. It might take the route of pilot implementation. The LPS roll out is based on experiences which at the beginning is supported by central staff units and external LPS experts and eventually is more decentralized. The responsibility of process improvements normally delegated to shop floor level. The last phase is the daily operation and continuous improvement that involves maintenance and continuous improvement of the designed process. It may be appropriate to mention here that in Taylor's scientific management, the knowledge and labour were strictly separated where workers were obligated to execute the process that management had designed. In such a system of decentralized work, continuous improvement cannot play out. In LPS this separation need to be eliminated, and a sustainable adaptation in daily operation is achieved in

LPS. The principles, methods, tools are deeply understood at all levels including shop floor workers. Hence, it is a distribution of information, which calls for identification, acquisition, development, transfer, application, and preservation of knowledge, crucial for implementation. Generally, knowledge depends upon the person who owns it and is a prerequisite for purposeful action. However, the question worth noting is, how to structure, organize, and manage the knowledge of an enterprise and what should be the approach to knowledge management? The process of continuously creating new knowledge, disseminating widely through the organization and embodying it quickly in new product services, technologies and systems is defined as knowledge management. Briefly, knowledge management can be described as process that creates, disseminates, and embodies knowledge. Understanding the transformation of knowledge is imperative to understanding the flow of knowledge for which classification of knowledge is of interest. Nonaka classified knowledge into two categories, one being the Tacit knowledge and the other as Explicit knowledge. Explicit knowledge is the knowledge that can be framed verbally, written down, stored, and the possessor or the person knows about it, can communicate it and also it is easy to transfer the explicit knowledge through data processing. While on the other hand tacit knowledge is complicated to formulate and transfer as it is based on personal attitude and experiences and is expressed by the person's belief and behavior. Technical skills and LPS knowledge can be tacit because the person possessing it might not know about it or is not able to formulate it. The four possibilities were recognized by Nonaka to transform knowledge from one type to the other. Tacit knowledge can be transformed into explicit knowledge by way of externalization because the tacit knowledge gained in the form of experiences and impressions are written down, and thereby are externalized. Socialization is just another way of such a transfer, whereby tacit knowledge is transferred without any transformation and this can happen irrespective of any specific language. Children learn from parents imitating their behavior. Explicit knowledge can be transferred either by internalization or in combination. Internalization occurs when the explicit knowledge is applied over and over and gets planted in person's habit and daily routine. Combination is a process when new knowledge is gained by integrating isolated explicit knowledge in a holistic system. The person who is responsible for knowledge management needs to know whether it is mandatory or optional or whether formal or creative for an organization to adopt. The barrier to knowledge that occur to manage and transfer it comes possibly from the individual or collective barrier and could either be caused by structural or cultural reasons. The complexity of the Lean transition is multiplied with the vast amount of information and knowledge available to the enterprise. It seeks support and assists the consultant to train their employees to incorporate in the whole organization. The flow of knowledge normally is invisible and can occur as intended or unintended between nodes. A node can be a member of a team as a role, and roles are an important part of LPS implementation. That allows describing knowledge flows, responsibilities and tasks without knowing the actual person. Knowledge flows start and end at roles that can operate from sender to receiver and the description of such knowledge flow have three crucial attributes- direction, content and roles. Therefore, knowledge flow is initiated by the sender and integrated by the receiver. With increasing levels of details, the knowledge gets more adapted to specific situation. The information contained in a message decreases with the increase of the portion to be determined. In the analysis of various LPS implementation, it is seen that knowledge flow differs widely and the affected roles are on the lowest level of details. Roles are the nodes in knowledge flows and are not bound to a specific person, but can be described by the tasks, responsibilities and their authorities concerning decisions. Roles are common in Project Management organization and with analysis; some found its application in LPS after matching of the set of roles with the known tasks, responsibilities, and authorities at the beginning of implementation. Recent implementation process focuses on sequence of tasks but seldom describes the process of implementing the relevant knowledge in the organization. The efforts to the development of measurement of LPS and the assessment of degree of leanness of manufacturing firms depend upon a model. It comprises of nine variables of Leanness-elimination of waste, continuous improvement, zero defect, just- in -time delivery, drawing of materials, multi functional teams, decentralization, integration of functions, vertical information system, using data analysis to measure leanness and agility of a manufacturing system. Financial and non-financial measures, excess inventory, transportation costs and defects, may be considered in assessing lean performance.

In conclusion, dynamic knowledge opens the path to innovation and contributes to the growth of organization. For the purpose of knowledge-creation process, an integrated dynamic knowledge made up of SECI requires consideration with a view towards improving the efficiency of knowledge creation. It reduces the knowledge gaps, but assists the future projects to start from a higher level of knowledge and helps in making the right decision quickly for faster and improved quality products. It also assists in reducing costly rework at the back end of the process by creating knowledge at the right time and at right place. A strong Lean mindset that fits into the organizational culture is important that require organizational changes to systems, practices and behaviour.

☐ The unique wage payment model in India

A unique form of wage payment in the gold jewellery sector seems, by all accounts, to be based on the wage-loss (or loss-wage) mechanism. It shows up when this cost is passed on to the worker as wage. This wage is not proclaimed or declared and has nothing to do with the minimum wage pay permitted by law. The loss of gold for the producer is a gain for the worker. The producer pays this wage-loss to the worker at about 4-8 percent of the product, locally called 'unit'. The rate differs between producers to producers. It is settled through a pre-assigned contract between the worker and the producer. In this arrangement, the workers are viewed as a strategic player in the labour market to achieve a higher rate of wage-loss, while the producer's strategic behaviour is always to pay the worker a lower rate of wage-loss. At times the producer needs to pay a higher wage to the worker in wage-loss payment than in monthly payment. The producer endeavor to pass on this loss to the consumer at the stage of final consumption in the retail price. The major determinant of the monetary wage loss is quantity, quality, variety and market price of the finished jewellery.

In understanding wage loss mechanism, let us assume that a final consumer puts in an order to the producer. The wage is counted on the finished product and is calculated in production on a unit basis. The real money wage is determined by multiplying this unit wage by the ruling market price of gold in the local market. The wage is connected with the changes in the market conditions and fluctuations in the market prices. The producer now pays this wage in monetary form to the workers. The division of labour in the production process and the money in rupees is ideally distributed between the workers' involved in the production activity. The exact percentages of the wage-loss depend upon the quality of the worker as far as skilled, semi-skilled, unskilled, and the quantity of work done. A skilled labour force may exercise larger bargaining power in the labour market and end up earning higher rate of wage-loss from the producer. The producer enjoys the gap between the money wage-loss in the first instance, and the unit wage-loss in the second. The producer will in general pay the worker a lower rate of wage, thereby accomplishing a net profit. But it is a net wage loss for the worker in his wage component. The worker naturally focuses to extract a higher wage from the producer through competitive bargaining to achieve a net wage gain. The producer consents to pay higher wage-loss rate if the worker guarantees larger number of orders and agrees to produce for the principal producer through his own contacts in the market. The quantity, quality and variety of the finished jewellery, considered three major determinants of the wage loss, swings in the same direction as that of quantity produced. The higher is the level of production, the higher is the wage loss given by the producer to the worker. As the division of labour dominates the production of jewellery items, the significance is reflected in the recruitment of workers of differentiated skill types at various stages of production. It is to be noticed that the percentage of wage loss declines with increase in mass production. If a worker produces in a large quantity under the same owner, the owner offers a lower rate of wage loss. The percentage of wage loss declines from around 6 percent to 5 percent that has made this mode of wage payment popular among the gold jewellery workers. They favor this type of wage structure, endemic to unorganized characteristics of the sector, as it provides them with opportunity to earn higher wages than regular monthly money wage payment. The producers agree to pay the wage loss during the contract else they might face a deficiency of skilled worker at the workplace.

Despite the fact that the workers are not organized and unionized, regardless they take part in the labour contract market in absence of adequate supply of skilled labour and the producers are constrained against migration of skilled workers to make the job rewarding for labour employment. The wage determination and fixation of wages in the organized sector has absolutely no bearing on the informal unorganized production sector of the Gems and Jewellery industry. Without effective mechanism for settlement of wage determination and settlement of disputes, the industry has evolved an informal method of operation in the loss-wage model. The establishment of this model has mitigated the industrial relations challenges, and in some measure the dispute resolution over wages, prompting significant gain in production capabilities, despite very little gain showed in labor welfare, worker health, well-being of family, child labour, education and their general working conditions.

☐ The idea of Hallmarking

One of the oldest forms of consumer protection believed to exist even today is no other that we know as "Hallmarking". Back in the year 1300, Goldsmith's company Assay office was with an intention to regulate the trade and craft of goldsmith. Edward 1 then passed a law requiring items of precious metal offered for sales to be uniform in quality as that of the coin (silver currency) in circulation. In this context, the goldsmith company Assayers was tasked to visit workshops in the city of London to assay silver articles and if they were found below standard and have less than 92.5% minimum silver content, were either destroyed or forfeited by the king. This led to a term that came to be known as "Assay Test".

When articles passed assay test, it received King's mark of authentication, the Leopard's head. Edward III granted Royal charter in 1327 to the company, and as the number of articles increased over the years, the merchants had to bring their articles to the Goldsmith's Hall for testing and marking, and then came to be known as Hallmarking, struck with King's Mark at Goldsmith's hall, which is its origin. The goldsmith company adopted the king's mark as their own town mark and the Leopard's head as the mark of London Assay office that now tests and hallmarks millions of articles of gold, silver, platinum and palladium every year. Hallmarking expanded its services to jewellery trade, offering variety of specialized analytical test procedures using latest technology coupled with traditional chemical methods and analysis. Earlier the test was known as "Fire Assay Cupellation test" that involves refining the pure gold content from a gold alloy by separation of the base metal from precious metal and gravimetrically determining the gold content by weight. In this, samples containing gold are analyzed by fire assay technique to determine their content. The sample material is mixed with lead oxide and flux ingredients in a crucible and fused in a furnace. The fusion process reduces the lead oxide to lead metal and alloy with the gold. The molten lead then collected in a mould, allowed to cool and then recovered. The resulting lead contains all the gold. This stage is followed by cupellation in which the recovered lead from fusion stage is heated on a magnesite 'cupel' to absorb the molten lead and waste impurities namely copper, leaving gold lead on the surface. Gravimetric analysis of the lead determines the other essential features of the sample. This established process requires great precision by laboratory technicians and meticulous recording of results at each step. Often this method is used for high degree of accuracy by competent analyst. The limits of accuracy is in the order of one of 1: 50,000 parts (0.002%) on a homogenous sample. Today the assay offices use a combination of techniques of analysis equipped with modern methods.

These include Touchstone testing that offer partial quantitative information about precious metal alloy, fire assay, X-ray fluorescence Spectroscopy, Potentiometric titration and ICP-CES. These are supplemented by highly sensitive analytical balances that can weigh up to six to seven decimal places, which reduces the analysis time, improves the accuracy and assists by expanding the sample size and types for analysis. The method for testing articles for hallmarking has improved with technology over time. From traditional hand marking with hammer and punch to automatic presses and now with Laser marking, that cuts into the item or etches a high degree of definition in either 2D or 3D that can be positioned and applied on any surface ranging from 0.3 mm to 0.6mm. Introduction of XRF machines as predominant test method, a large number of items are processed quickly and non-destructively for Hallmarking. XRF's accuracy of measurement has proved to be as good as fire assay method as a reference. The cupellation method is considered the most accurate method for testing fineness of gold alloy in most cases. These days XRF instruments that are used are energy-dispersive XRF's that offers to measure thickness of coating and its chemical composition of homogenous material. The accuracy depends upon the quality of the test sample. Statistical sampling and samples from an item are both integral part for determination of fineness and the accuracy of the result is dependent on sampling, surface area, spot size, homogeneity, solder free test areas, apart from the ability of the instruments to resolve the elemental spectra produced by fluorescence. This instrument when fitted with silicon drift detectors offer excellent energy resolution and high count rates that are ideal for near elements such as gold, platinum, iridium.

105

There is emergence of new protocol to be designed and later adopted to produce responsible gold with the support of LBMA, WGC and Responsible Jewellery Council. The concept of responsible gold evolved because of use of mining in the Democratic Republic of Congo (DRC) and adjoining countries, and its potential revenue that resulted directly or indirectly finance or benefit armed groups in those countries to undermine legitimate governments. Post 2008 crisis, the Dodd Frank Act of USA put a requirement on US companies to ensure the use of gold, among others, only from legitimate sources. This puts refiners to establish an audit trail from mining to refineries, which basically is to provide assurance to end users ensuring that the gold produced has a clear history and complies with the Dodd Frank Act.

Another fast emerging venture is E-scrap (electronic scrap) recycling resulting in gold extracts from obsolete electronic device such as Smart-phones, Tablets, either or with other precious metals such as silver, platinum, and palladium. The Waste Electrical and Electronic Equipment (WEEE) since 2003, with directives from European union, has imposed e-waste recovery and recycling targets on IT and electronic industries with penalties for companies and member state for non compliance. In 2012, WEEE has made manufacturing legally and financially responsible for safe collection and disposal of the old equipments. The 25 states of USA passed legislation, requiring e-waste recycling, and covering around 65 percent of population according to Electronic Take Back coalition. This may seem to be economically efficient, apart from environmental positives, to recycle tones of smart phones as opposed to many times the weight of gold ores and could stand out to be a potential business venture in the days to come.

The hallmarking of gold jewellery and related products are required to be done in India to determine accurately, the proportion and purity of precious gold in the metal. It is the mark that is used in many countries to guarantee the fineness, basically, the purity of gold jewellery. It has been introduced under BIS Act 1986, but on voluntary basis, wherein the license is issued to the jeweller for certification of purity standard specification-IS 1417, that is a scheme operated through network of regional offices across India, where any jeweller has to approach the recognized assaying and hallmarking centre to get the product or article hallmarked. The idea is to protect the consumers against possible purchase of substandard, non-compliant under caratage articles, and to be able to develop a culture and business environment of quality for export competitiveness. Essentially, it provides assurance, confidence and satisfaction to the consumers regarding quality of gold jewellery for a given price so that he is not victimized. It offers opportunity for filing complaints if purity is found to be less. In 2008, government of India made hallmarking compulsory, but it was not followed rigorously. In February 2011, government of India implemented BIS (Revised Act, 2011) and inserted a provision of penalty if not implemented. Whereas, jewellers having BIS license are required to provide commitment, assurance to quality, ensuring purity of gold jewellery, developing a system of quality assurance in operating hallmarking scheme, displaying all the requirements needed for describing the components of hallmarking and finally providing customer satisfaction.

The five components of BIS mark are Fineness number (caratage), Assaying or Hallmarking centre's mark, Jeweller's identification mark and year of marking denoted by a code letter decided by BIS corresponding to the year. The marking is done using either punches or laser marking machines. For a licensee, a jeweller, a manufacturer or a retailer, there exist a need to apply to BIS for use of standard mark (Hallmark) on their jewellery. Once the license is granted, the jewelers are required to register with BIS recognized Assaying & Hallmarking Centre to get their jewellery hallmarked following the approved scheme for certification. BIS maintains surveillance on the certified jewellery at a defined periodicity that involves collection of hallmarked gold jewellery for licensee's retail outlet or manufacturer premises and test it for conformity in BIS recognized Hallmarking centre. In the event of any deviation in the degree of purity or non-performance to the system, it may result in cancellation of BIS license that invites legal proceedings for penalties under BIS rules and regulations. Hallmarking of gold jewellery is done based on the conformance of the jewellery regarding declared purity and is returned within 48 hours. The officials of BIS visit the Centres periodically for the purpose of verification and recognition of hallmarking Centres that are renewed every three years upon satisfactory performance. In most of the advanced countries, after production, jewellery is first hallmarked before displaying it on the shelves of the retail shops. This culture in India will take some time and is evident to mature only when the demand for every piece of jewellery, required to be hallmarked, matches with the growth in number of hallmarking Centres across India to sustain the load, covering the entire rural areas, which might definitely take some time to evolve.

☐ The distribution channels in jewellery industry

The jewellery products are moved from producers to the consumers through channels of distribution. Such organizations that facilitate the distribution of products are the channel intermediaries. The specialized functions that they perform enable manufacturers to make their goods according to the consumer requirement. Channel of distribution maybe defined as a marketing channel that has a structure of intra company organization, units, company agents and dealers, wholesale and retail, through which a commodity, or a product or a service is marketed. A channel is the pipeline through which product flows on its way to the consumer. The product is put in the pipeline or in the marketing channel and various people move it along to the consumer located at the end of the channel. The number of intermediaries making the distribution channel has number of stages, and the channel length and its associated complexity depends upon range of functions required. The effectiveness of a distribution channel depends upon the efficient movement of such products and its lien from production to consumption.

The marketing channels and structure in jewellery industry that flows in the pipeline have several channels. One is from manufacturers to wholesaler then to commission agents to retailers and finally to consumers. The manufacturer approaches the wholesalers to sell their newly designed jewellery. The wholesaler may approach the retailer directly or through commission agent as per indication of customer liking and satisfaction. In this framework, jewellery can be manufactured as per customer specification and need. Second channel involves the manufacturers cum wholesalers, who produce in large quantity as per the latest trend, taste and preference of the customer. Sometimes commission agents are deployed to find potential buyers in the retail market. In turn the commission agents looks out for retailers in the market and procure orders from them and in this process they are found to establish a healthy relationship with the retailers and offer them products desired at a reasonable making charge. The commission agents are committed to their commission and not on profits. This marketing channel is found to have some popularity in urban, sub-urban and rural areas. The Third marketing channel or structure visible in India is an open sale of jewellery in the market in which jewellers directly get familiar with the retailers to display their new designs so as to bag orders. Often these orders are booked by the consumers as per their own choice and then jewellery is manufactured. This system is not found popular in the urban areas as against sub urban areas, and particularly in rural area, they are found to be less popular. The Fourth channel in the structure comprise of manufacturer of smallholdings, who are very popular in rural areas, in quantity, and have less option in trends and design wherein one can demand for manufacture of personalized design needs as the manufacturer has limited capital to hold stocks. The Fifth marketing channel normally adopted in the interstate distribution is based on sending agents to seek for orders by showing designs, because carrying high value jewellery has an associated market risk. This structure holds true for specific product like chains that have product-oriented demand. These items are known by its popular names according to designs and are sold outside of any specific geographic area for wide consumption of the entire quantity manufactured. The sixth channel involves manufacturer of branded jewellery who use this structure to save charges paid to the marketing intermediaries wholesalers, commission agents, and retailers. The branded companies have their own research laboratories, manufacturing workshops and produce according to latest designs and consumer preferences. They have the opportunity to display designs on their own websites to seek attraction of the consumers. Normally they exist as open retail outlets at central locations of cities in the country.

Marketing channels consideration and structure at international arena is understood to exist in export and import of products. While international market conducts business activities that direct the flow of goods and services to consumers at more than one country. It involves different consumers of varied needs, desires and tastes. In drafting a strategic distribution channel, independent countries with its own legislations and regulation in foreign trade involve internal and external institutions, legal binding commitments and obligations to other firms and individuals in the respective countries. The export-marketing channel requires less documentations when compared to domestic marketing channels. The common international channels that we get to see are as follows - The manufacturer comes in contact to local export agencies or any other authorized agents who deals in specific jewellery articles or products. The domestic agencies having contact with foreign intermediaries send the specifications to their counterpart abroad. The foreign agencies thereafter collect orders from the retailers or customers in their own country for the required quantity. After fulfillment of the legal procedure for importation of the product, the exporter then executes the manufactured items taking necessary care for the packaging needs.

Manufacturers of jewellery are increasingly getting aware of export of their products to foreign countries. They are showing keen interest to get in touch directly with the export import agencies abroad to market their products. The urge to compete in the international market has the advantage of cutting the margins of the intermediaries. They send designs and specifications to seek orders and finalize the deals. These products are sold in the various outlets of the importing country to reach to the customers. This phenomenon is gaining popularity because of more transparency and margin factors.

Beneficial ownership in the age of AML/CFT
and the revenue model

The Financial Action Task Force is an intergovernmental body comprised of 37 members which sets internationally recognized standards (FATF recommendations) to address Anti-money laundering (AML) and Combating Financing of Terrorism (CFT), and proliferation. It leads a global network of 198 countries who have committed to implementing the FATF standards. They have agreed to review and evaluate their level of technical compliance and their effectiveness. The main aspect of FATF standards is the Beneficial Ownership, which remain a key focus in its review of analogous countries and related follow-up processes. In the past, actions were taken to facilitate transparency and provide access to beneficial ownership information on legal persons in a time bound manner in consideration to its legal arrangements.

The International standards on beneficial ownership focused on legal requirements of financial institutions and other related authorities to collect and verify information on the ownership of legal persons and arrangements, and on such measures as to ensure that reliable information is available to the investigators. In 2012, FATF offered clarity about how to ensure availability of information amongst countries and how to address vulnerabilities, bearer shares and nominees. The revised standards seemingly distinguish between basic ownership information about the immediate legal owners of a company or trust, and beneficial ownership information about the person who ultimately owns or control it. Having accurate up-to-date basic information about a legal person or arrangement is a fundamental prerequisite for identifying the ultimate beneficial owners and requires countries to provide international cooperation relating to ownership of information. To facilitate, FAFT issued guidance on transparency and Beneficial Ownership in 2014, which clarified on the required standards that stepwise guide to access publicly available information on corporate, and how to establish procedures to facilitate information when requested from foreign counterparts. The FATF issues necessary guidance papers to assist financial institutions and other authorities and gatekeepers to implement FATF standards, including beneficial ownership requirements. A report placed before G-20 in July 2016 observed the existence of large-scale misuse of legal persons and arrangements and identified the need to strengthen control against the misuse of corporate structures. It becomes imperative for the countries to effectively implement FATF standards and close the gaps in the national systems about legal persons and arrangements. Simultaneously, the global forum, an offshoot of OECD, adopted the Automatic Exchange of Information (AEI) Standard, which incorporated the beneficial ownership information as well, and requires financial institution to report on beneficial ownership information to their tax authorities for onward exchange in relation to financial accounts. The decision to apply peer pressure to countries for fast implementation of FATF standard, made many countries to put in place sound legal framework requiring financial institutions and other related authorities to collect beneficial ownership information on customers (that is legal person legal arrangement) . It may be stated here that the role of FATF as a body, that have a global network, is to assess compliance with beneficial ownership requirements, in the context of implementing AML/CFT measures. While Global forum OECD is an assessment body to assess compliance with beneficial ownership requirements as they apply in the context of transparency and exchange of information for tax purposes.

Both these organization are responsible to give clear and consistent recommendations on how to improve the implementation of International standards on beneficial ownership for AML/CFT and tax purposes.

☐ Indian way to deal with Financial Action Task Force

On 25 June 2010, India turned out to be a full-fledged member of the Financial Action Task Force (FATF), an intergovernmental body, in charge of setting the worldwide standards on Anti Money Laundering (AML) and Combating Financial Terrorism (CFT). India earned membership because of recommendation of compliance and mutual evaluation report in the plenary at Amsterdam, Netherlands. Since 2006 India remained as an observer at FATF body. It was essential for India in its desire of turning into a major player in International Finance. It will help India to enhance its ability to fight terrorism and trace money laundering, illegal tax avoidance, and terrorist financing offenses. India will benefit in anchoring more stable transparent financial system by guaranteeing that the Financial Institutions are not defenseless against infiltration or abused by organized crime groups. The FATF procedure will help India in coordination of AML/CFT endeavors at an international level.

The Prevention of Money Laundering Act (PMLA) 2002 came into effect in 2005 and was amended in 2009. The Unlawful Activities Prevention Act (UAPA) 1967, was altered in 2009 that criminalized terrorist financing. It was revised in 2008 to expand scope and bring more enactment that pursues prerequisites of United Nation Convention for the suppression of Financing of Terrorism warfare (FT). As a pioneer in developing economies in Asia, it faces a range of ML and TF dangers that originates from illegal activities perpetrated inside and outside countries that includes drug trafficking, forging of currency, fraud, transnational organized crimes, human trafficking and corruption. ML techniques are diverse and common in opening multiple bank accounts, blending criminal proceeds with assets of a legitimate origin, obtaining bank cheques against cash and steering through complex legal structures. Internationally it exhibits the use of offshore corporation and trade based tax evasion. However, India has a mechanism in place to address such trends, and periodically formulates appropriate response. Since 2009, India expanded its emphasis on ML provisions even with essential long-standing legal issues like threshold conditions for domestic predicate offenses that requires attention and whose effectiveness relies on ML convictions. A few preventive measures have been taken according to FATF standards and a few remains to be implemented. Supervisory necessity for financial institutions is sound. However, its effectiveness is not adequately illustrated. The recommendations made to India are in favor of addressing the technical deficiency in criminalization of both ML and TF and in the domestic system of confiscation and provisional measures, widen Customer Due Diligence (CDD) commitment with clear explicit measures to upgrade the present requirement of Beneficial Ownership. It looks to improve the reliability of identification document, the use of pooled account, the Politically Exposed Person(PEP), by internet-based business. It seeks to explore the Indian office's AML/CFT compliance, improve adequacy of Suspicious Transaction Report (STR), the changes in sanctioning regime that takes into consideration effective proportionate and dissuasive sanctions against inability to agree AML/CFT requirements. It considers extending PMLA to DNFBP (Designated Non-Financial Businesses and Profession) like casinos, guaranteeing that they are adequately regulated and supervised. Some of the institutional measures are effectively taken for India has criminalized ML under both

PMLA Act 2002 as revised in 2005 and 2009, and the Narcotic drugs and Psychotropic substances (NDPS) Act 1985 as amended in 2001, though PMLA is applicable to most of the extensive range of predicate offenses, including opiates and cross-border implications. In 2009, it has been in accordance with FATF guidelines. Significant improvements are expected in the system for sharing information between Directorate of Enforcement (ED) which investigates the ML offenses and Law Enforcement Agencies (LEA) which is responsible for investigating the predicate offenses has been institutionalized and the 2009 amendment permits registration of predicate offense instantly, facilitating parallel concurrent investigation of ML. With the combined application of Section 15,17,40 of the unlawful activities (prevention) act 1967 as amended in 2004 and 2008, India has made important move to meet the International standards, governing criminalization of terrorist financing. India is involved with all treaties annexed to FT convention. Despite of the fact that numbers of technical inadequacies that exists should be routed to make it more aligned to FATF standards. The confiscation regime in India takes into account a wide range of seizures and forfeiture measures in the AML/CFT setting, that isn't completely extensive and has technical deficiencies that to a great extent affects the jewellery industry. The definition of proceeds of crime and prosperity in the PMLA are broad, and sufficient enough to allow for confiscation of property derived directly or indirectly from proceeds of crime allowing for confiscation of corresponding value, paying little respect to the property whether held or possessed by a criminal or an outsider. The UAPA does not take into account full equivalent value of confiscation. The effectiveness of the confiscation provision made under PMLA, NDPS Act and UAPA, can't be assessed because of the low number of confiscation. However, India has sufficient framework for freezing terrorists related assets.

The Home Ministry has issued rules laying out the procedures for implementation of freezing assets directly. The financial sector regulators RBI, SEBI, IRDA have issued guidelines to banks, stock exchanges, depositories, intermediaries, and insurance organizations concerning the obligation to act predictably with freezing mechanism. The authorities issued guidelines for DNFBP sector but there are no evidences of effective implementation. Apart from the financial sector, no appropriate measures are in place to monitor compliance with relevant enactment and guidance to force sanctions against non-compliance. On November 18th, 2004, Government of India set up a Financial Intelligence Unit (FIU) reporting directly to Economic Intelligence Council (EIC) headed by Finance minister. It became operational in March 2006. Aside from the central national agency for receiving, processing, analyzing and disseminating information relating to suspicious financial transaction, FIU-IND is in charge of coordinating and strengthening efforts for national and international intelligence, investigation, and enforcement agencies in driving worldwide effort against MLTF and related crimes. It considers a legal basis of investigative techniques that allows for undercover operation, interception and different types of surveillance. India uses a combination of declaration system about FEMA that uses currency declaration forms(CDFs), and a disclosure system that applies to currency and Bearer Negotiable Instruments(BNI) carried by incoming and outgoing person through Indian ports. Restrictions are in place on sending currency through post and cargo. In PMLA rules, numerous brochures and guidelines are issued by the regulators to be covered by the FATF standards that are set up for compliance. Nonetheless, India's record keeping generally conformed to the prerequisite of the FATF guidelines of February 2010 amendments to the PML rules having rectified most of the previous deficiencies.

India has established compliance to cross border wire transfers and financial institutions that considers large complex transactions of uncommon patterns. The PMLA rules covers institutions to report to the FIU, all cash transactions greater than INR 1 million (US Dollar 20000) or its equivalent foreign currency or altogether for a month that does not surpass threshold limit. Money service business and foreign exchange houses that facilitate cross-border money transfer are to be licensed by RBI under FEMA and Payment and Settlement Systems Act (PSSA). Most Valuable Liquid (MVL) sector was brought into AML/CFT regime from 1 June 2009, however, a sizeable informal sector is operating illegally, the scale is in fact unknown. There are breaches found by ED in the Hawala type transactions. The designated non-financial business and profession conducting business in India includes Casinos', attorney, land operators, bookkeepers, company secretaries, gold merchants in valuable metals and stores. These businesses are not subjected to PMLA provision aside from Casinos. It is to be seen in light of absence of clarity and disparate practices in connection to identification and verification of beneficial ownership. The professional secrecy provision prevents identification of beneficial ownership of client account.

☐ The idea of preventing crime while increasing revenue

The precious metals and stones have been linked to corruption, smuggling, illicit financial streams, arms, drug trafficking and financing of terrorism. It is believed that if the trade in precious metals and minerals are overseen legitimately, it provides opportunity for increased income. This presents necessity of staff expertise in battling AML/CFT that demands specialized support and analytical advice on management of resources. Most importantly, Precious Metals and Stones (PMS) are appealing to criminals and are being used in AML/CFT. Some of the attributes that make PMS are diamonds, emeralds, sapphire, rubies and metals like gold, silver, platinum and comparable metals that seems to be attractive to legitimate buyers. They are worth for their high value, compactness, durable, untraceable, odourless, tradable in cash, can be held secretly without a need for records and considered as a safe investment. Diamonds have a high value which is directly proportional to its weight and gold is easy to melt and can be cast in any shape. These properties make them the most splendid items. Precious minerals and stones have displayed opportunities to be smuggled from producers to consumer countries that often finance armed conflicts or maintain a strategic distance from domestic taxation. The real value of the production often remains undeclared to the authorities so as to minimize the tax exposure. The high value offers opportunity of bribe at every level of official checking in the extraction and trading process. The returns of smuggling and corruption are laundered. PMS are purchased with illegal funds generated by either drug or human trafficking. PMS are used in trade-based money laundering (TBML), as a cover for laundering unlawful funds, created from different violations, by price manipulation or false invoices that cover fictitious sales of PMS. The proceeds are passed off as having been generated from genuine buying and selling of PMS sources. PMS are used as an alternative currency for buying prohibited or restricted goods such as gold for cocaine, diamond for weapons or as a means of storing of wealth by illegal activity and maintaining a strategic distance from seizure and confiscation.

In some countries in the Sub-Saharan Africa, PMS is a noteworthy contributor to countries GDP while in some countries despite of larger production and reserve of PMS, the official statistics of exports income report exhibits well below actual levels. It is seen that under performance of such economies results in failure of government to collect revenue related to informal nature of the small-scale sector in mining and trade. Often poor governance is the principal reasons in the conversion of natural resources so as to pursue development that is sustainable. The tendency of secrecy in PMS matters and its typical characteristics of high value, portability, and odourless, render it making of a closed environment by the limited number of wholesale buyers, all the more so as in diamond. For implementation of AML/CFT measures in the financial sector, especially in developing markets and developed countries, where financial institutions and banks are involved in PMS trade, the inability to meet FATF guidelines and recommendations for customer due diligence (CDD) procedures have brought in low compliance. The proper definition recommended by FATF in its "Risk Based Approach" (RBA) guidance for PMS dealers, include range of actors from miners to intermediate buyers and brokers, polishers of stone to retail seller and those operating in the secondary and scrap markets. This definition determines all the different categories of persons subjected to AML/CFT prerequisites, that have direct relevance for PMS which includes FATF R.1-that offer "risk based approach" that allows national authorities to allocate more resources to the monitoring of PMS sector where identified country pose a high risk level. FATF R.22-requires PMS dealers to implement CDD measures having specific relevance to any cash transaction equal or over the applicable threshold limit of US/EUR 15000 where PMS dealers are required to know their customers and gather adequate information that establish transactions to be legitimate. FATF R.23 - requires PMS dealers to send Suspicious Transaction Report (STR) to the authorities.

The suspicious activity is normally reported to FIU, set up by law to analyze. FATF R.28 - calls for regulating and monitoring the dealers of PMS by compliance of requirement in AML/CFT measures. Customer due Diligence (CDD), record keeping and reporting are the new normal. In this, criminals and associates are prevented from accreditation, licensed or beneficial owner of a critical or controlling interest in holding a management function in PMS dealership. FATF R.32 - is set up to detect cross border transportation of cash and bearer negotiable instrument are PMS, and persons carrying such items are subjected to declaration or disclosure requirements. FATF R.34 - is intended to offer guidelines and feedback by authorities and their supervisors to the PMS dealers. The FATF recommendations, AML/CFT, and standards offer relevance in entirety to detect, deter, and prosecute crimes and laundering proceeds of crime related to PMS. It can confiscate proceeds related to mining, tax evasion, smuggling, corruption, including financial service sector along with combating predicate crimes. It is important to make reference to FATF R.32 that concerns cash couriers, yet recognizes PMS to combat smuggling. The FATF did exclude precious metals and stones for purpose of recommendation in regards cash couriers, yet recognizes PMS as 'high liquidity' and in use as a means of exchange for transmitting value. Especially when a nation finds abnormal cross-border movement of precious metal or stones, it is required to be notified to appropriate custom service or other competent authorities of the nation from which the item originated and to establish source, destination and purpose of movement of such item and appropriate action. It is not required in FATF norms, but a country may keep PMS as a part of declaration or disclosure system alongside currency. PMS offers a source of 'rent for official' and a possible instrument for laundering in the process of corruption.

121

Through CDD mechanism all financial institutions and DNFBPs are expected to ascertain whether their customers have a high exposure to corruption risk or the alleged Politically Exposed Person (PEP) holding senior positions in government, military or judiciary. When exposed they need to go under enhanced due diligence measures and are required to be reported to FIU. The corruption risks involving PEP and PMS originate by purchasing PMS and afterward PEPs endeavor to launder the proceeds, generated by illicit sale of PMS. Often PEPs ask for special facilities at Financial Institutions as safe deposit boxes to safeguard precious metal and Stones. FATF 26 and 28 requires competent supervisors to ensure that FI and DNFBPs are not directed or controlled by criminals or their associates and those persons are not beneficial owners of the controlling interest or the management function in such institutions.

Implementation of AML/CFT framework leads to formalization, licensing or registration of dealers with expanded transparency in transactions, which results in tax laws to be less demanding to enforce. The competent authority needs to have an adequate power of monitoring and sanction combined with sufficient technical and other resources to play its functions. This has probability for improved tax collection as the PMS sector is recognized as a major impediment to tax collection. Smuggling and tax crimes are viewed as predicate offense to money laundering that offers enhanced chances of revenue collection. Predicate offense to money laundering requires financial and non-financial institutions to report suspiciously transacted funds and proceed to FIU. Coordination and cooperation mechanism between AML and Tax authorities permit requesting relevant information held by FIU on a timely basis and in analysis of STR by FIU. The adoption of Risk Based Approach requires national risk assessment grants superior allocation of resources for effective mitigation. The three primary categories of risks affecting PMS are country or geographic risk, customer or counter party risks and finally the product or service risks. The available framework targets dealers who are at risk most and abused by MLTF. The forming of risk matrix comprising different factors to establish a risk profile of every dealer might be grouped into structural factors (size of a dealer, geographical location, ownership, corporate structure, years in operation, etc.). Some business specific risks are inherent (to be specific, Origin of customers, share of regulated customers, quality of minerals traded and so on) components that mitigates the risks (adequacy of ML/TF risk management system and controls). When the risk profile is built up, it will aid in supervision, planning and in conducting inspections. Synergies with different supervisors of PMS administrator lends effectively in monitoring the dealers. It is apparently basic to establish synergy that have International dimension of RBAs, to target countries of interest for international cooperation and to harness the knowledge of producing country of PMS to trading countries of both legitimate and unofficial channels. Developing a helpful arrangement between risk prone countries or jurisdictions is of vital interest.

The RBA in revenue administration and AML/CFT implementation can possibly prevent leakages through tax evasion, smuggling and corruption. This requires PMS actors in this sector to assess ML/TF risks faced while implementing measures to identify dealers in the sector, Record Keeping and STR prerequisite, supervision of the segment, controls on cross border involvement of PMS, which helps tax administration in enhancing tax payer base. Modern tax administration dwells on voluntary compliance and self-assessment, as their resources seem to be limited. Categorization of PMS, whenever split into large, medium and small taxpayers, and when well directed, yield better revenue collection. High rate of tax, complex policy framework, illiteracy and inability to understand complex systems drive small taxpayers out of the tax system. High compliance costs suggest similar outcomes, but are not a problem of compliance for large dealers. Hence, it makes it easy to comply for the PMS, increases tax obligations and the education tools and services along with guidance helps in compliance.

☐ The idea of VAT packed in the name GST

The basic principles of value added tax (VAT) designed to tax final consumption in jurisdiction where it occurs according to destination principal, has continued to spread all over the world in the international trade of goods and services, in an increasingly globalised economy. Since 1990s, tax authorities and business community have come to recognize that VAT rules require greater coherence and cooperative approach to solve common problems. OECDs notable work in this area with Ottawa conference on electronic commerce in 1998, have endorsed the Ottawa Taxation Framework conditions, enabled adoption of the guidelines on Consumption Taxation of Cross- Border Services and Intangible Property in the context of E-commerce (2003) which matches and harmonizes with the Consumption Tax Guidance Series.

Evidence grew that against strong growth in international trade in services, tax issues needed attention beyond the electronic commerce, but VAT has the potential to distort cross border trade in services and intangibles that was creating an obstacles to business activity and hindering economic growth with distorted competition. The VAT system interacted continuously across jurisdiction requiring facilitation. OECD launched a project to develop International VAT/ GST guidelines. For reducing the uncertainty and risk of double taxation and non-taxation resulting from inconsistencies in VAT application across borders, the guidelines sets a path in terms of principles for VAT treatment for most common International transactions on trade in services and intangibles among stakeholders. These guidelines sought objectives and suggest means for achieving outcomes, and merely serve as a reference wherein sovereign countries are left to the design and application of their own laws by their policymakers who could evaluate and develop the legal and administrative framework in their countries, and consider economic, legal, institutional, cultural and social circumstances and practice. Governments were expected to shape an effective tax framework while assessing the likely effects, costs and benefits of policy system, ensuring flexibility of responding to evolving circumstances and demand that calls for revision of guidelines.

Essentially, the VAT deviating system, in whatever name or acronym, known as GST, must embody broad-based taxes on consumption collected from business through a staged collection process, but not theoretically to be borne by businesses, irrespective of the approach whether being a invoice credit method or subtraction method. Taxes that lack these features are outside the scope of the guidelines and are not applicable to the single-stage consumption taxes, charged at the final point of sale, as retail sales tax. Businesses have to bear the compliance costs associated with the collection of tax at all intermediate stages of supply chain up to final consumer thereby collecting and depositing tax to the tax authorities, are considered as key partners in the countries process operating the VAT system and its development of framework. Apart from the core principles of VAT, the other main principles that apply to cross border trade are the neutrality of tax, the definition of place of taxation for cross border trade in services and intangibles between businesses and final consumers and mechanisms for supporting these guidelines. Traditionally, that include cooperation, dispute minimization and its application in evasion and avoidance are of paramount interest. The core feature of VAT comprise a broad based tax on consumption by household, private individuals, and not businesses, engaged in consumption at which VAT is targeted and VAT regimes have to determine the extent to which the purchase is treated as acquired for business purpose or for private consumption. The staged collection, control and remittances in the supply chain correspond to its margin. The difference between VAT imposed on taxed inputs and tax output and in principle tax is collected on the 'value added' at each stage of production and distribution. This relieves businesses of the burden of VAT paid in acquiring good and services or intangibles and thus permitting successive taxpayers to deduct VAT they pay on their purchase and account for the VAT they collect on their sales. Under invoice credit method or transaction-based method, the trade charges VAT at a specified rate for each supply and passes to the purchaser an invoice-showing amount of tax charged. Thereby purchaser is able to credit the input tax against output tax charged on its sales, remitting the balance to the tax authority and receiving refund out of excess credit. This design feature offers VAT in domestic trade as neutral tax. VAT, therefore, flows through the business to tax supplies made to consumers. VAT as levy on final consumption and its staged collection process has a bearing on international trade of whether it should be improved by jurisdiction, country of origin or of destination. Under origin principle, the tax is levied in various jurisdictions where value is added, but in destination principle all firms in a jurisdiction are placed on an even footing competing in a given jurisdiction rendering neutrality in international trade.

In international trade, exports are not subjected to tax and involve refund of the input taxes or "zero rated" and imports are taxed on same basis as the rates for domestic supply. The total tax paid relating to supply is determined by the rules applicable in the jurisdiction country of its consumption and the revenue accrues to the jurisdiction where the final consumption occurs. In contrast, the origin principle allows revenue to be shared in the applicable jurisdiction where the value is added which potentially could influence the economic or geographical structure of the value chain and undermine neutrality in international trade. The reason of widespread acceptance of the destination principle for applying VAT to international trade, majority of the rules currently in operation are generally intended to tax supplies of goods, services and intangible within the jurisdiction where consumption takes place. To make an export free of VAT systems that operate on invoice credit method, the VAT on cross border business-to-business supplies of goods and services are collected by Reverse Charge Mechanism. This tax mechanism switches the liability to pay the tax from the supplier to the customer. In absence of such mechanism, foreign suppliers that deliver services in jurisdiction where they are not established in principle have to register for VAT purposes and fulfill all the necessary VAT obligations in these jurisdictions. To avoid such administrative burden on foreign suppliers, and to ensure that VAT is accounted for, the reverse charge mechanism allows or sometimes requires the VAT registered customer to account for tax on supplies received from foreign suppliers. If the customer is entitled to a full input tax credit with respect to supply, it may be that the local VAT legislation need not require the reverse charge to be made. Though the reverse charge mechanism is not applied in all jurisdictions and wherever implemented, the rules may differ from country to country.

The widespread consensus in the destination principle as international norm is sanctioned by WTO rules, based on which India's GST framework is aligned so as to match with the local needs and enable it to become representative.

☐ GST Guidelines and its implications on Gold jewellery in India

The rate of GST applicable on gold bullion and gold jewellery is the same as the rate of three percent. When bullion is purchased GST will be applied once at the rate of around 3 percent and when it is converted into jewellery, there is another GST on forward supply of such jewellery. As per schedule published on 03.06.17, all precious metals, precious and semiprecious stones (other than rough diamond and precious, semiprecious stones) are to be taxed at the rate of 3 percent. Rough stones are to be taxed at the rate of 0.25 percent. For imports, the 3 percent rate of levy equivalent to IGST will be on the Basic customs duty. Concession or Exemption for imports under GST is allowed for commercial samples up to 3.0 lakhs in value in case of Gem and Jewellery and not exceeding 50 units in number per year imported as a personal baggage by bonafide commercial businessmen or imported by post or air. Re-import of cut and polished precious and semiprecious stones sent abroad for treatment are exempted as well.

For the purpose of levying tax on imports of the precious metals such as gold or silver, the Basic Customs duty (BCD) is considered on tariff value fixed by Government by notification (sec 14 (2) of customs Act). As per section 5 of IGST act, tax equivalent to IGST will be levied on imports provision of Sec.3 of Customs tariff act., that is tax payable on transaction value plus BCD or on Tariff value plus BCD for gold/silver. The gold purchased from nominated agencies will be a taxable supply and GST at the rate 3 percent will be payable by

Nominated agencies. There is no exemption under GST for inputs used for export purposes. Export can be made under the bond without payment of IGST and refund of unutilized input tax credit (ITC) can also be claimed. Alternatively, export may be carried out paying IGST and thereafter rebate can be claimed. Most importantly for exports, provisional refund of around 90 percent will be granted prima facie satisfaction within 7 days of exports and the remaining 10 percent within 60 days after scrutiny of the application and other documents such as Shipping bills, invoices, FIRCs etc. In the performance of export shipments in the name of manufactures, principal manufacturers and traders, a large array of activities take place in the domestic market. This has reference to artisans or karigars, as a business entity, their making charges, labour charges and administration of provisions of GST application with respect to supply destination. Further, the documentation, HSN within state, intrastate, registered, unregistered, input credit, branch transfers, manufacturer, principal manufacturer, valuation and treatment of GST on such activities leading to export performance and compliance in terms of record and traceability (reverse charge, composite scheme, registration) E-way bill, exhibition. The services of skilled artisans who make jewellery if engaged on principal to principal or business to business is taxable, but if they are directly employed by the principal then they are not taxable under GST. A very important concept called "reverse charge mechanism" operates in the GST regime from the supply side for tax neutrality point of view. Normally, the liability to pay tax is on the supplier instead in reverse charge mechanism the liability to pay tax is transferred to the recipient of supply or any other designated person . Reverse charge is applicable for goods. If recipient of any supply of goods or service from an unregistered GST supplier, the registered person who receives those supplies, is liable to pay tax under reverse charge, and hence import of service falls under reverse charge as also other supplies as notified by government. There is no threshold limit (INR 20 lakhs) for reverse charge and the recipient is liable to pay tax for any supply. Here the tax paid under reverse charge can be taken as ITC, subjected to restrictions, as well as under taking of related compliance under GST. The services taken from unregistered job worker by registered dealers are required to pay tax on reverse charge basis. A notable point of Karigar's being 'supplier of service' cannot opt for composite scheme. If the Karigar, who supplies service is below Rs. 20 lakhs threshold limit, and is an unregistered dealer (NRS), the recipient needs to pay the tax directly to the government under reverse charge by the way of issuing an invoice for the supply. [Sec 31(3) (f) read with rule 1 of the invoice rules]. The recipient needs to issue a payment voucher when making payment to the Karigar. Recipient needs to pay the tax under first reverse charge and then adjust the credit after going through the usual process of showing the tax paid under reverse charge in the Returns, since there is no auto adjustment mechanism. It is to be understood that there is no limit to "Reverse Charge Mechanism" and it is only applicable to recipient of supplies from all unregistered person. The format for purchase from URD is same as usual tax invoice format. In reverse charge scenario, the tax is to be paid as per the time of supply of goods or the date of payment entered in the books of accounts of recipient or depending on the date of debit of payment or within 30 days of date of issues of invoice. The above rules are applicable for advance or part payment. Normally, under GST, in the event of supply of goods, the time of supply is considered as date of issuance of invoice, last date of issuance of invoice or last date of receipt of payment by supplier. Whereas in supply of service it is date of issuance of invoice or date of payment whichever is earlier in case if the invoice is issued within prescribed time. But if the invoice is not issued within prescribed time, then date of provision of service or date of payment is earlier and in all other cases the date on which the recipient shows receipt of services in the books of account. It is of interest to note that any advance received are liable to GST and it arises when the payment is received by the supplier.

The place of supply for import is considered as a location of the importer and for exported goods it is the location outside India where the goods are exported. But where supply involves movement of good in such a case it is the location at which the movement of goods terminates for delivery to the recipient and where movement is not involved, the place of supply is the location at the time of delivery to the recipient. For supply of service in business to business it is location of the recipient, and for business to customs it is location of the recipient where address on record exists, else location of supplier. In the event of repair services, GST is to be paid only on labour charges at the rate of 5 percent. Repairs that involve supply of goods and services, separate bills have to be prepared for the goods at the rate of 3 percent and for services at the rate of 5 percentage. All job work in relation to cut and polish diamonds, precious and semi- precious stones or plain and studded jewellery of gold and other precious metals is taxable at the rate of 5 percent with full input tax credit (ITC). Job work is treated as a "supply of service" and GST charged at the rate of 5 percent and if the turnover of Karigar exceeds a threshold limit of INR 20 lakhs and INR 10 for special category states, GST will be paid by the Karigar. When the Karigar is not registered, the GST will be charged by the principal recipient under reverse charge mechanism.

In this arrangement, the principal can send goods and inputs to a job worker without payment of tax, under intimation and subject to condition as may be prescribed under Sec. 143 of GST act and procedures wherein capital goods and inputs have to be received back within 1-3 years. In the event of carrying further specific job on the jewellery it can be sent to another job worker without paying of tax. If the goods are not returned to the principal manufacturer within required period of time, it will be deemed that the goods were supplied to the job worker originally sent and the principal is liable to pay the GST along with interest prescribed. The documents prepared in relation to job work are Delivery Challan (Rule 10(1) b of invoice Rule), E–way bill wherever applicable (Rule Electronic way bill rule) along with proper accounts of inputs and capital goods, semi–finished or finished goods, received from job worker to be maintained by principal (Sec-143 (2) of CGST Act, Rule 1 of Accounts and Record rules).

The goods can be cleared directly from the premises of the job worker in such situations where the premises of the job worker is registered as an additional place of business of the principal manufacturer or the job worker is registered under GST Act. There are certain goods for which the Commissioner may notify that the principal is not required to register the job workers premises as an additional place of business. The waste and scraps can be removed by the job worker if the premise is registered else by the principal. In the event of redoing the work lacking satisfaction, the same will be treated as normal job work that will follow the same procedural and compliance requirements. When the job worker charges for re-doing the job over and above the charges of the original job, additional GST will be payable on the charges of the job preferably within one year period. When a principal manufacturer give wastage and making charge for any job work to an URD, it will primarily be evaluated on case - by – case basis. It is understood that making charges will be liable to GST under reverse charge. The tax liability on reverse charge will be considered for discharge. This will depend upon whether the quantum of wastage offered to the Karigar impacts the amount of making charges. In such a case the waste has to be included when paying the GST under reverse charge. But if it can be shown that the wastage does not impact the amount of making charge, then it may not be included when paying GST under reverse charge. It has to be remembered that when the unregistered job worker's place of business does not have any occurrence for sale of goods or dispatch of goods to customers from that place, there will be no requirement of mentioning the premise as an additional place of business.

It is apt to consider the fact that there is no provision of any centralized registration under GST administration in India. Registration, if so required for operation of a company may be obtained in each state separately even for CGST to establish consumption of supplies and is valid throughout the state. Even when goods are supplied at the exhibition venue in another state where the supplier does not have any office, a need to obtain registration as a casual taxable person under GST that is required to make an advance deposit of the likely GST that would be payable. When the goods are transported for exhibition purposes, and not for the supply, the goods are then taken to the exhibition venue under a delivery challan as no other document is prescribed currently. If the possibility of no sale exists, then there is no need for registration of casual tax person as no supply of goods may take place.

Another element worth considering while transacting and generating invoice is the application of Harmonized System of Nomenclature (HSN), an internationally accepted system for classification of goods, in order to establish uniformity in identification of the goods through a code. Though customs and excise use the 8 digit classifications, but for GST a maximum of 4 digit code has been adopted.

The input services related to Gems and Jewellery sector that are taxable under GST and rated and that qualifies ITC, can be classified in 3 categories. Services consumed in terms of rent / premises, Hallmarking / Certification, Advertising, Housekeeping /Maintenance, Sales and Exhibition, Vaulting, Security, Banking, Insurance, Software, Legal attracts 18 percent GST while travel logistics at the rate of 5 percent (no ITC) and Transportation at the rate of 12 percent and Marketing at the rate of 5 percent, however, offers full Input tax credit. In general Input tax credit (ITC) is available in respect of goods and services used in the course of furtherance of business. ITC is available only when the supplier has paid GST to the appropriate government. Certain categories of ITC such as motor vehicles will not be available so is construction cost of immovable property but it is available for plant and machinery. The statement and returns needs to be filed by the job worker having aggregate turnover of above INR 20 lakhs, which are details of outward supplies by 10th of the following month, inward supplies by 20th of the following month, Monthly return by 20th of the month including outward or inward supplies plus any rectification of entries along with GST payment details. The Annual return consolidating the details for the entire year needs to be filed by 31st December of the financial year.

CHAPTER 3

Future challenges in Jewellery industry

☐ The challenges that mostly come from within

I

ndia's gems and jewellery industry is primarily unorganized due to the fact that more than 90 percent of the players tend to inherit family owned businesses from their ancestors. This somehow is because of the love that the Indian consumers have for traditional art of gold jewellery and not to forget, the legacy the sector embodies. An observable shift in demand and taste of the current generation shows a required push towards the sector to get organized. Despite the move being of glacial pace and moderate; the future holds promises largely because of the adjustment in lifestyle and preference of the customers. It is much simple to consider the unorganized sector responsible for turning into an excellent provider of jewellery products. However, very little interest exists as to why the industry remained unorganized for such a long time regardless of the industry performing so well. A study by FICCI on gold jewellery industry indicates that there exist around 450,000 goldsmiths, more than 100,000 gold jewellers alongside 6,000 diamond stone-processing players and 8,000 diamond jewellers in India. At the same time the business remained to a great extent unorganized, which poses a challenge, that still remains a serious constraint preventing the advancement of the industry into an organized sustainable sector.

It is realized that the gems and jewellery industry relies upon imports for its raw materials supply, some part of which is processed into finished products for domestic consumption and the rest for exports. The rough diamonds, precious and semi precious stones, precious metals like gold, silver and platinum are imported as raw material. The challenge to this industry comes from factors such as unpredictability in price of raw materials, supply side constraints from mines, exchange rate fluctuations, currency wars, geopolitical circumstance and from elements concerning economic cycles of sovereign nations that influence the demand supply equations. The changing demographics of developed countries of the west with aging populace, and the rise of emerging markets with young populace gradually tends to tilt the seat of demand from developed country to a rising new class of consumers from the East. This is set to change the worldwide trend in marketing landscape that requires an adjustment in fashion of gems and jewellery, especially for high prices of diamond, gold and silver. The exporters don't have an adequate design development Centres to innovate the latest designs that matches with the changing trend of the foreign buyers. The manufacturers tend to make the appropriate gems and jewellery products as per the market demand. With the changing trend the demand for the product starts to decrease ultimately leading to a slack situation. This circumstance tends to block the manufacturer's capital that seats in the huge stock pile. The producers give the stock to the brokers for selling. The producers reduce the cost of production to half and the sellers reluctantly sell their items at a lesser price.

Employees and workers are a critical aspect of any industry. The labor force in Indian gems and jewellery sector is less productive in comparison to China, Thailand, USA, UK, Sri Lanka and Israel. The non-availability of skilled workers is persistently referred to as one of the significant reasons behind the inability of the leaders in this industry to scale up their operations. The supply of artisans or craftsmen that comes through generations should be supplemented by fresh talents, trained in a professional way, to have access to a much wider talent pool. The industry has seen a remarkable increase in shift from metal to wax techniques. Metalworking, mould making and setting are unmistakably more difficult than working with wax where the need of skill and time are both desired. The exporters are confronting scarcity when it comes to availability of workers skilled in metalwork. The industry's on-the-job training model needs longer training time thereby creating gap in availability of industry related best practices and standardization fundamentally in the fragmented part of the industry.

The prices of gold and silver, have witnessed some increase, over the recent years, which results in changing the purchasing behavior of consumers. Within the period from December 2008 to December 2009, the price of gold per 10 grams, has increased from Rs.13,445 to Rs.16,870, an expansion of 26 percent (Bose, 2011). Despite the fact that the price of silver had demonstrated a decline after February 2009, it again began to rise after April 2009. From Rs.17,847 per Kg in December 2008, the silver price has increased to Rs.27,430 per Kg in December 2009. In December 2013, gold for each ten gram was Rs.30221, and Silver for Rs.44223 per Kg. Indian gems and jewellery (G&J) sector has been principally affected by the imposition of different government regulations, rising gold prices, rupee depreciation and languid GDP growth globally including India. With rising and volatile gold prices, the demand for gold jewellery, gold bars and coins will start to decline. To reduce the rise in Current Account Deficit (CAD), a slew of measures has been adopted by the government to curb the gold imports. These regulations adversely affects the industry by increasing the working capital requirements, constraining the gold supply in the short term, creating a hike in the gold price and reducing investment demand for gold. The lull in the global economic growth chiefly in US and Europe is believed to affect the growth of emerging countries like China and India.

India right now enjoys dominance in the world's cut and polished diamond market. China may develop as an opponent in the long term because of the availability of cheap labor, growing domestic demand, and improvement in the quality of workmanship in the country. It is worth noting that an expansion in the number of diamond processors are setting up their facilities in China for these reasons. There has been a growing pressure in major diamond processing nations like Africa, Botswana, Namibia and South Africa, to gain economic advantages from diamond value chain, thereby looking for investment in cutting and polishing industry. Such developments may influence the prospects of India. An increasing number of diamond processors from Israel and Belgium, and even

India, are setting up offices in China, primarily because of cheap and disciplined work force, huge increase in potential consumers in the high-income segment inside the country and the steady improvement in quality of Chinese workmanship. Technology is an area where the Indian industry faces a long-term threat from China. China because of its cutting edge and automatic production lines has succeeded in creating a favourable position for itself to fabricate jewellery at competitive price.

The exporters are constantly confronting with difficulties in accessibility of low cost financing. The short-term bank credits like cash credits, letter of credit with interests ranging from 10 to 15 percent appears to be expensive to exporters as the raw material costs are high, leading to financing challenges for jewellery dealers. In gems and jewellery industry most of the stones bargains are expensive. The exporters require more finance for investment. There are different issues faced by gems and jewellery exporters when it comes to sourcing their capital. The high rate of interest charged by the banks on export credit, lack of dollar credit for sourcing of rough diamonds and precious metals, less sanction on expansion of credit limits of gems and jewellery exporters, presence of negative bias in rating of gems and jewellery firms by Credit Rating Agencies (CRA), and formalities of financial organization are being exceedingly tedious process to name a few. Transportation is important component of the gems and jewellery industry in India. Exporters in gems and jewellery industry confront with issues of not being able to fulfill the demand of products. They try to fill the absence of any professional organization or government counter. This forces them to get raw material of gems and jewellery as indicated by their necessities. Export is a basic hardship. The clearance of parcel from custom and different formalities takes much time and after the dispatch of parcels, it reaches in the foreign countries in 5 days. To overcome this issue, exporters dispatch their parcel from Delhi that enables the parcel to reach the country concerned within one day. The parcel of such a precious object is not safe. Another challenge faced by the exporters is the low level of research and development (R&D) intensity and facilities for undertaking research and product development. Proper R&D solutions would lead to enhancing the product quality, reducing wastage, introducing new designs and concepts, and innovation in supply chain management and marketing. The gap between high-end machines and unskilled labor can be reduced with inventive R&D solutions.

☐ Doing business in India digitally

The agile hands of the young people in India are waiting to seize the opportunity for potential engagement in occupations that characterizes the Indian demographic advantage which is broadly published, and prepared for dividends and profits. The path to Foreign Direct Investment in different sectors is made ready. It is one thing for foreign companies to bring in funds for investment in India but another to operate businesses in India that requires global organizations to learn the art of doing business in what we call as the Indian way.

India's divided market in the digital space constrains companies to embrace multiple channels for transferring active calls or data sessions (cell in a cellular network onto another) from one channel to another. The existing labor laws make distribution costly. The distribution operation to entrepreneurs when contracted out reduces the costs and raises the market penetration. The commitment to country or region should be visible by requirement of local talents and empowerment of local operation. The challenge that rises out of customization of local market need includes question as to-What is there to offer to the market?

Whether joint ventures could be a correct approach or simply parting and going alone is the ultimate solution.

India is growing at an average rate of 6 percent that poses a tremendous potential for the white merchandise sector to grow rapidly for a considerable length of time as is seen in the mobile sector. The commitment to country specific operation and management system and the capacity of global companies to ride through the India's economic cycles and unpredictability could be an advantage as opposed to being entrapped in profitability and lack of commitment. The absence of giving away autonomy may put companies to face hierarchical and bureaucratic barriers in its managing while at the same time putting resources into talents, empowering decisions on capital spending and product pricing, holding local managers accountable, which will in general create space for faster development and execution of strategies. This will thereby assist in concentrating resources and enhancing faster decision-making process that enables the organization to serve the local customers in a better way and further enabling the organization to grow rapidly. The local empowerment needs to penetrate the lower level of the management that assist in the drive for innovation, entrepreneurism on the ground and reduced time for marketing new products. It is clearly no big surprise that the right people, in the middle management level, are exceedingly critical to the successful execution of the growth strategy. With the developing professionalization of Indian organizations, the strong productive managers would not have much incentive to work for in a branch and the position requires offering entrepreneurism, greater authority and incentives. It must therefore be recognized that leads to advancement of a culture of meritocracy, accelerated career paths, fair and transparent advancement process, and performance based system to motivate self-starters and incentives differentiated for high performers. The structured rotation of strong performers, offers mobility and customized leadership program, leadership development courses that prove effective for recruitment and retention process. The global organizations comprehension of India in the diversification that exist within the sub continent, includes both have and have-nots, that have varied dialects, education, and geography from the stance of rural and urban divide, offering challenges to companies to meet customer satisfaction. This is despite the fact that the challenges from local competitors are no less.

The Indian consumers tend to place demand on sophisticated modern products and services available in the advanced countries however at low price. This approach offers competition from localized products and services by means of innovative business models and process. This implies working with the local suppliers can lessen the cost that enables offering of less expensive prices to end consumer and customization that draws a potential game changing strategy. (TV with menu in local dialect). The "Design to Value" approach has progressively picking up significance as far as "Frugal Engineering" is concerned, which in turn is a capability in which talented employees are rotated in product development process that could be reasonably priced and innovative. Joint Venture approach is often thought of at the entry level of the market having a local partner to proficiently navigate the market complexities and oversee regulatory issues. The limitation of joint ventures is that it underscore on short-term performance over long-term goals, commitments and alignment of interests of partners control and transparent path of ownership. A strategic alliance with local players is a key element in consideration.

There emerges a need to talk about some of the trademark characteristics and attributes associated with successfully doing business in India. Above all, the top leadership support and commitment through the business cycles must be guaranteed while setting bold aspirations over next five years to accomplish fivefold growth. In this course of action, taking part in regular dialogues with best customers and keeping up appropriate level of local investment through business cycles are essential to commitment. It is important to gain profound understanding of some target customer segment and draft such initiative that drive fivefold growth. The market share goals are to be set for the target customers tailoring the products or service packages to the client segment needs, taking into consideration the local market difference that proposes customized offerings to suit Indian markets and client needs. To be successful in India, there is a need to create innovative and localized business models that commit to products that have less functionality, which costs less without compromising on quality. The models must cover building distribution network that suits target customers and expansion plans. It needs a provision for robust supply network in India with dependable vendors conforming to the quality specifications To scale up through partnerships and deals, it is required to assign a business development team for Merger and Acquisition that scours for opportunities periodically in India. Overseeing results proactively each and every quarter in case of developing strong partnership with joint ventures is something desirable. The need to leverage for acceptable pan India products, services and talent requires formation of team for research and development with adequate resources to deliver results, advancement of business models and technical innovation for relevant markets that consider benefits from local cost advantage, scale and talent pool. The management of perception and regulation has turned out to be vital in these perplexing webs of activities. This offers to maintain strong association with the stakeholders, government and regulators, rather than depending on external agencies. It is required to position the brands that achieve premiums in areas over local competitors, while ensuring that the brand has adequate local attributes.

Since all exercises are coordinated and performed by people, convincing suggestion to empower local organization is fundamental. This could be accomplished by pulling out senior officers in All India board, providing CEO's with their own budget and autonomy for everyday decisions, monitoring career development for officers in advisory group, recruit leaders from pan India operation and achieve reputation as a preferred employer.

The above discussion is relevant and material to any white goods company of global stature and scale, including jewellery chains, that are willing to make a foray into Indian market with an intention to become successful.

☐ Jewellers need to accommodate in the era of digitalization

Emergence of the markets to deliver digital content and services offer new and exciting opportunities in abundance in the digital market space through internet sales channels. A study by McKinsey states that in India, around 65 million people are using cell phones, which ranges approximately between 180 to 200 million further creating a drop in the use of PC only. The use of PC and mobile was 16 million which got decreased to 15 million. This just implies that the use of Web-Via mobile phone has increased opening doors for companies to roll out wired and wireless broadband network with the goal that use of advanced smart phones network are more affordable which will require development of new content type. From this study, it is inferred that Indians spend on an average four hours out of every day in devouring online and offline products. Consuming videos, downloading videos and online music, potentially will generate heavy traffic. The use of best services may be overwhelming in the near future and so the mobile medium seems to be an effective and optimal way to fill the gap. The major factors that can come in the way are the hardware and equipment cost, inconsistent network, quality and limited access. The area of mobile content and social services are set to change. There will be creation of offerings that are simple to access and its use will require editing and marketing in local languages. The content may involve voice and single touch mobile internet access to overcome the aspect of illiteracy combined with lack of delivery clarity especially in the rural areas. There will be the requirement of efficient payment systems for profiting from the content, which frequently affects the essentials for the development of a legitimate revenue system, beyond consumer access and services. There may be a need for selling regional and local advertisement in local dialects on cell phones for easy acceptance, clearness and understanding. There will be a need to monetize by balancing cost of the materials with the goal to reflect the value of the content, delivered in real time and in specific contexts of shopping coupons received through mobile devises as customer passes through certain stores. Mobile content and services can be relied upon to improve with the end goal of public services to deliver information incentives, similar to healthcare mechanism, management of business, through word of mouth. All these activities tend to create employment for artificial intelligence skillset by applying statistical analytics to read the positive contents about a company and conclusions on leaders in the web-based social media space. The business have to manage social media crisis, identify the source of negative posts, devise measure that can counter the

145

unleashed substance of the contenders from where it started. To do this, the content must fundamentally be user friendly. Something like jewellery, which when published daily on a dedicated website, that ought to be viewed as an entertainer such that Jewellery will be a main part of the story line. There could be an approach to distinctly run a storyline mounted with initiatives, which could include the blog, to generate searches through live online chats. It is known that people anticipate responses with every post. A need to build up a process to engage effectively with individuals in a way that communicate brand identity, values, consumer concern and does not lead to negative viral spiral. There has to be a reliable mechanism to check the performance of the social media as well.

☐ Rating Agencies that rest on conflict of interest
and unaccountability

In the financial system, rating agencies play a critical role in providing an independent assessment on the creditworthiness of debt issuers. This allows market players to make informed decisions in financial and capital markets that offer liquidity to corporate in the economy. The ratings of companies give a fair idea about the company that seeks to borrow money from the market (in terms of either a pension fund or money market fund) to invest in company's bond. Today, the role played by Credit Rating Agencies (CRAs) have come under severe criticism and public scrutiny. Studies have suggested that the rating agencies have knowingly inflated the credit ratings of financial products with a goal for profit and market domination. Sometimes even ratings of countries get downgraded on unsound parameters that often put financial markets of that country into uncomfortable position raising question about the integrity and accuracy of such ratings. This is possible in absence of national and international regulatory framework which are dominated by a few rating agencies namely Standard and Poor's, Moody's, FITCH. The policymakers have recognized the need of regulatory response post the 2008 financial crisis. A series of regulatory interventions affecting the rating agencies, that are advocated by G20, are called for a strong supervisory oversight over rating agencies.

The Credit Rating Agencies usually offers grades based on the performance of debtor's bonds and other debts, like bank loans, that are used in investment decisions that turns out to be important when it comes to management of both corporate and countries credit risks. It is an opinion regarding credit-worthiness and quality of an entity, its financial obligation, debt security, preference shares and other financial instruments. An issuer of such debts and instruments uses a defined ranking system of rating categories. The publication of independent, specialized, assessment on debt issuer's credit-worthiness by the CRAs, reduction of the information costs between the lender and the debt issuer, helps improving the number of potential investors to promote liquidity in the market. CRAs provide independent, standardized third party assessment of quality for the creditworthiness and credit risks associated with bonds and financial instruments that gauge the ability and willingness of an issuer to meet its financial obligations fully and prompt. This can be depicted by using a letter grade ranging from 'AAA' to 'D' to communicate opinions relative to level of credit risks and likelihood of default. The grades slightly vary between CRAs but broadly represent categories to indicate similar credit characteristics. The first four categories are investment grade 'AAA' through 'BBB' ratings of S&P and FITCH.(AAA through BBB for Moody's considered good quality with AAA+ represents highest credit quality and BBB-represents lowest investment grade credit quality). The

AAA ratings is immune to any risk apart from cyclical shocks like Great Depression, BB and below are 'Speculative' grade meaning that the company or issuer currently can repay but may face with uncertainties. The lower ratings indicate significant chances of default. There can be revision of letter grades ratings after periodic revaluation at intervals. These ratings are used for short term or long-term investments and business decisions, and no guarantee is attached. Having no accountability of guarantee on investments, these rating agencies have accumulated enormous reputational capital over a period that has resulted in gaining investor's blind assumption on CRAs infallibility.

The credit rating agencies operate broadly on paid or unsolicited ratings. The revenue that it generated through paid service that either comes from the issuer on whose request the risk is assessed or from the subscribers who receives the published ratings and credit report. Historically, CRAs generate revenue by selling the information to interested investors through a 'user-pay' system, which shifted to an 'issuer-pay' model, wherein the rating agencies charge the issuers for rating their credit-worthiness. In this method risk is assessed and ratings are given at the request of the issuers of debt instruments. The rating agencies factor in their independent information with those obtained from issuers, which are not available to public. The ratings are publicly available free of charge by charging the borrowers of their service than the investors while spreading the cost of rating evenly across investors. Some others make assessment available only by subscription, essentially 'private subscription' services, under confidentiality agreement in return for a fee to access the agency's rating by large institutional investors. The unsolicited ratings are nothing but assessment of creditworthiness without involving the issuer and the assessment are shared with the public. In this, the public, individuals or institutional investors or the issuer of debts, companies or countries pay the agency for the ratings.

The influence and success of the rating agencies is due to the oligopolistic nature of the industry in an unregulated environment. The heavy reliance of national regulators on rating agencies outsourcing responsibility in calculating risk exposure and capital adequacy requirements, and it's insistence on third party credit ratings, gives explicit recognition to CRAs, which successfully creates in CRA a role of de-facto regulator in the financial market. Much of it is owed to rating agencies that have been around for more than a century since its founder John Moody credited with devising credit ratings in the beginning of 20th century. The rating agencies are always under criticism and scrutiny in case of any financial crisis because of their questionable revenue earning model, easy legal environment and unchecked role. Highly rated Enron, when found bankrupt, opened the eyes of the policy makers in USA leading to regulatory interventions. Subprime crisis and sovereign debts emboldened policymakers for fundamental modifications as the rating agencies were found enablers to the financial crisis. Investigations found CRAs to have misused role and influence over global financial markets in rating the inflated structured financial products, and downgrading countries rating. The inaccurate ratings led to mismanagement of risks for the Financial Institutions and investors hiding from them the actual risk in mortgage related securities and collateralized debt obligation. In its drive for high profit margins, so as to get more business, the rating agencies started overrating such structured products and consider these financial products lucrative and important to business when compared to traditional bonds. The competition between rating agencies and the corporate or sovereign countries, makes matters worse in rating agency shopping. Hence, rating agencies have incentives to issue top ratings regardless of whether such ratings are tenable. The rating agencies downgrades a sovereign country as below investment grade that puts financial market in a state of uncertainty that may encourage immediate liquidation leading to herd behavior. This increase market volatility and may cause asset price to reduce with uncertain financial stability, which not only affects the country but the entire financial system and the related market players. Such is the power and influence of CRAs. Some mechanisms were identified because of the need for regulatory response to reduce reliance on rating agencies. The framework attempts to scrutinize the methods conducted for ratings, the accountability of rating agencies, and reduction in reliance, corporate governance, establishment of institutional mechanism of supervision of rating agencies, and most importantly conflict of interest. The institutional response post the 2008 crisis, led by G20, advocates a strong oversight over the rating agencies through codes of conduct, that meets highest standards to avoid conflict of interest and may offer greater disclosure to investor and issuers, particularly differentiating complex financial instruments. The Financial Stability Board (FSB) in 2010, sets in motion certain alternative principles and standards of creditworthiness, and recommended market players, banks, investors to make their own credit assessment and not to rely only on CRAs entirely. FSB was authored to remove and replace all references to CRAs in laws, regulations with recommendation drawn from peer country review. Basel II and III Framework seeks to address over reliance of banks on rating agencies related risk assessment and securitization. The International Organization of Securities Commission (IOSCO) sets a robust code of conduct to guide CRAs regarding protecting the integrity of rating process so that investors and issuers are treated fairly. It makes attempt to address the CRAs issue of independence, conflict of interest, responsibilities to the investors and issuers along with disclosure requirements. In compliance with G20 mandate, IOSCO code is incorporated into national laws universally by all countries. Institutional framework for recognition, registration, supervision of CRAs which became an important step initiated along with the establishment of Security Exchange Commission (SEC) in USA, ESMA in Europe (European Securities and Market Authorities - system of financial supervision). These centralized institutions could initiate action through public notice, withdrawal of registration, and request SEC to impose penalties and fines. The challenge that remains is the 'issuer-pays' revenue model of privately owned rating agencies that entail a conflict of interest, and how too much of regulations play out in the agencies effort of being credible and non conservative in its approach to rating, and finally own responsibility and accountability with the investors interest in mind.

☐ The idea of Rating the Rating Agencies

Since 1999 the Securities and Exchange Board of India (SEBI) along with Reserve Bank of India (RBI), Insurance Regulatory & Development Authority (IRDA), Pension Fund Regulatory Authority (PFRDA) and others, regulated a handful of Credit Rating Agencies in India. The large-scale nonperforming assets (NPA) of corporate in India and subsequent failure of CRAs have posed a crucial question regarding reliability in rating due to widespread rating shopping. The persisting conflict of interest based on 'issuer pays' model wherein CRAs are dependent on issuers of instruments for the payment of their fees which offers scope for undermining of service to investors interest. The conflict of interest increases in CRAs employees having long-term relationships with issuers due to less competition in the industry. The employees at the lower rungs of the CRA organization, bound by service rules, rates and attaches notes of their typical observations and findings, to draw attention of the highly paid executives at the top end of the structure, that gets ignored and often overlooked as the revenue earned from the issuers are responsible for paying the lavish salaries of the top executives. This arrangement inherently makes the senior executive's position vulnerable, which is a perfect recipe to lose a chunk of business revenue if real transparent assessment is offered that does not protect the issuer's interest. In such a threatening situation, the decision makers at the top are prone to mellow down their observations. On top of it, those same senior highly paid executives, who find seat in the rating committee finally attests any ratings of an entity that are perfectly positioned to influence rating decisions. Unless alternative remuneration practice evolves, and rotation of employees undertaken, independence of individuals in CRAs is difficult to retain. It is worthwhile to mention that not much studies done and investigation made into the operating margins of the respective CRAs that swings wild and is capable to open up awkward questions. Rating of shopping is another practice observed in issuers who seek ratings from multiple CRAs and pays for highest rating that they disclose. SEBI requires CRAs to rate securities during their entire lifetime to prevent withdrawing of ratings except in extreme circumstances. Here the ground of withdrawal of ratings is an area that requires a careful approach. In consideration would be the ratings on established platform for material disclosures, which if displayed may reduce the separation of unfavourable ratings. The lack of accountability towards investors in lending reputational capital to issuer that impact investment decision is often ignored. The compensation to investors for any loss arising out of negligent or fraudulent rating is an area where adequate safeguard is desirable. The vulnerability in rating activities will remain in the securities market employed unless rating of instruments is covered appropriately other than securities. The difference in instruments like bonds and bank loans are not accounted for in making of regulation.

It is sufficient to note that the rating agencies have entered a new era of regulatory control in the discharge of crucial obligation to the investors and issuers. The enhanced measures have increased public scrutiny and disclosure of their conduct and methods. In large measure, it has reduced absolute reliance on CRAs limiting their role in the financial market. The structured products receive stringent restrictions on ratings. Internal governance and conflict of interest substantially reviewed but practice of 'user pay' method of revenue still remains to struggle. Considering rating agencies as a vehicle of prediction or expression of opinion may only reduce reliability whereas an expectation of making expert opinion by CRAs on reasonable ground, a representation in making agencies accountable for outcome of such representation. The future of credit rating agency will depend upon how effectively it seeks to overcome the legitimacy test. The strengthening of the existing system from the perspective of the investors increases the predictability while reducing the risk is probably the way forward. In the past decade, India has been struggling with its own credit failures. The corporate defaults are on the rise continuously. The businessmen are overly indebted and shutting shops to simply escape the country with whatever residual capital they are able to manage remain a fugitive which in itself become a business model now . This requires a critical examination of the financial system in operation in the country and all the associated process of regulation to be learnt from failures. The latest 'too- big- to-fail' of all is an Infrastructure Leasing and Financial Services (ILFS) company rated AAA (the highest rating by CRA) until ILFS defaulted on its huge debt. A credit rating agency is a company that rates debtors based on their ability to pay back their interest and loan amounts, and also to signify the probability of default. The credit ratings agencies made appearance in India in the late 1980s and those registered under SEBI are ICRA, CRISIL, and CARE. FITCH, SMERA and Brick Work ratings. The Securities and Exchange Board of India tightened the disclosure standards for credit rating agencies. It assigned ratings to companies and their debt instruments further directing that CRAs must disclose the liquidity position of the company rated. While assigning rating on assumption of cash flow, rating agencies are now required to disclose the source of funding. The rating companies are required to analyze the deterioration of liquidity and check for mismatch in asset-liability. Today, rating agencies need to declare their rating history and show how the ratings have transitioned in various categories.

The failure of ILFS that accounts for around 16 percentage of banking sector exposure prompted the regulator to review the rating standards. The disclosure of a company's financial situation and cash flows will help investors and fund managers to take informed decisions and prevent over reliance on rating agencies. The rationale in rating will increase accountability as ratings assigned need to be backed by strong reasons. The disclosure of history will be advantageous to the investors to know the quality and trustworthiness of the ratings. Again, too many disclosures for the rating on agencies may render them to be conservative in assigning the ratings, which may not be good for investor sentiments. The issuer- pays model is yet to look for a proper answer for rating agencies. The company's independence to select rating agency that look to raise debt or borrow may lead to rating shopping. The right to choose and pay a rating agency may always lead to the path of conflict of interest and oversight. Moreover, the high barriers to entry of CRAs prevents competition, which primarily protects the interest of the investors. Having less option of CRAs mean compromise in quality standards, which is less likely to improve. Finally, who rates the rating agencies and how to ensure their accountability?

☐ The coming opportunities in emerging markets

A new consumer class is rapidly developing in the emerging markets. The industrial revolution that happened in the middle of 1700 took two centuries to evolve. The Great Britain took 150 years to double its economic growth. In the second phase of industrial revolution, USA took 50 years to double its per capita Gross domestic product. India took 12 years to double its Gross domestic product while China took 16 years. The main contrast between countries is that the two India and China began with 1 billion people, which is ten times more than that of England and USA collective populace that comprise of 10 million people. A study in the year 2010 uncovers the fact that the best 100 largest companies headquartered in developed countries gets around 17 percent of aggregate revenue from emerging markets and that includes 36 percent of global Gross domestic product. It is expected to contribute a hooping 70 percent of global Gross domestic product in future.

The long-term growth of global economy complimented by urbanization offers capabilities of development with the removal of trade barriers and in adopting market oriented economic policies. It is anticipated that growth would double the consuming class to more than 2.4 billion people, in which it is estimated that migration to the cities would be around 4.2 billion people in the following upcoming 8 years out of the aggregate near global populace of 7.9 billion people by 2025. The yearly consumption is relied upon to rise to $ 30 trillion from the

10 trillion in 2010, which is relatively half of total global Gross domestic product.

The electronics and white goods industries are expected to drive the greater part of the global demand. Another consumer class have risen in the digital age, the greater part of its users are in the emerging markets. As the E-commerce online business and the mobile payment system gradually spread across remotest corner of the villages, this will enable emerging market consumers to shift to the digital transformation. The triumphant consumers from the emerging markets, nurtured by the developed nations, will require an extreme change in mentality, abilities and resource allocation. The emerging markets consumer preferences will drive the global revolution in product design, manufacturing, distribution, channels, supply chain management and the likes. This will require targeting of urban growth clusters, for exclusive growth, recognizing precisely the balance, the local relevance and scale that will decide in formulating market segment strategies. Tanishq, a local company has been able to build a fast growing jewellery business, stressing on local designs and payment options that offer choices to communities and regions. Any company that tries to offer essential products or services to compete with low cost local players and try to allure customers requires innovation and localization, while redesigning product lines, service operations and supply chains.

The brands that build in trust that resonates needs to assume a significant role in deciding emerging market consumers. In the emerging markets, around 63 percent of population is under 35 years of age and the prospective new customers, who purchase a vehicle, TV, or refrigerator perhaps for the first time experience. In the exceptionally divided retail space that offer little consistencies in product introduction and promotion, the struggle for new choices of the prospects, as they move from country sides to urban communities, grasp new ideas and ways of living that offer them their own identities. They are extremely sensitive and receptive to effective branding efforts and switch brands freely. They will in general focus on the initial consideration that favours brands that have high visibility and trust. Building of trust requires investigation of brand message and delivery. The campaign for reliability is very compelling. The mobile and digital channels, similar to E-commerce, are positioned to offer additional opportunities to construct trust and awareness to brand. In India, consumers are grasping mobile devices, and low education among consumer enable them voice activated websites and services. The digital marketing should be a coordinated campaign strategy across a range of channels, including imminent promotion and educational campaigns. To control the market it is important to consider factors that impact the customer decision, desire and experience. That could be a challenge. The fragmented and unorganized nature of the retail field in the emerging markets, combined with limited e-commerce penetration, drives the buyers to 'mom and pop' shops regardless of whether they need to reach the small outlets by negotiating bad roads, controlled by multi level distribution network of salespersons and wholesalers. This gives local retail leaders the benefit of longer relationship with customer base complimented with low pay.

India in its early stage of economic development with less urbanization is comprised of 3500 towns, 334000 districts in 29 states and 9 union territories. Considering the fact that by the year 2030, almost 73 percent of nations Gross domestic product is anticipated to come from the 10 states and 62 percent of urban population, concentrating on 12 clusters around India's 14 largest cities that can possibly give 60 percent of nations urban Gross domestic

157

product. This comes out to be a distinct advantage for companies planning ahead of time to optimize on supply chain, sales and marketing network, while gaining from lower customer service costs of 5 percent to sales against around 10 percent. The other option might bring into focus on those states where average consumer earning is around 2.0 lakhs every year, which is more than the all India average that demands micro marketing strategy. Normally in developing markets, the growth starts from large number of consumers who try new products, and with the maturity of markets, the growth is supported by consumers who buys more goods and services and will in general purchase costlier versions of the products that they already have. This buying pattern will in turn hold back the basic necessary product categories. The health and wellbeing sector will witness much growth, while mid segment necessity items like apparel and household products are expected to appear above average growth. The brands that are centred on mass-market appeal are to be repositioned to go with the rising aspiration. The next decade is relied upon to observe a few classes of consumers who have their very own sense of difference and individuality. The companies will require distinctive value proposition to connect with each group and stand out in competitiveness. This will arise a need to position the brand or auxiliary brands to target a thin consumer segment that offer more tailored value proposition. The brands available across many consumer segments will in general struggle as far as prices defending their market position. To maximize and interface with consumer segment, they will be required to adopt and create a range of brands and secondary or associate brands to amplify on their brands range.

☐ A glance at the future decade

A large number of experts generally have a view that precious metals will remain relatively high because of conditions of demand and supply and recognize the fact that gold is money, which is inversely related to the value of benchmark dollar, and plays out the function of hedging in difficult economic times. At the back of emerging countries continued development and growth with respect to that of conventional developed economies, the jewellery market in BRICS is ready to grow and alter the economics of manufacturing. In the area of designs in jewellery, fashion and luxury goods, Italy and Europe does not see any other countries to peep it past and may continue to be market leaders in spite of the challenges from overseas competition especially in high quality product and design. The ethical sourcing of materials, precious metals and gems, are not considered as 'conflict materials', and will assume a predominant role later on as the idea of 'green jewellery' picks up in the value chain from mines to market pipeline. The green jewellery made out of sustainable, accredited materials will be found widespread, making a push for accreditation schemes for gold and diamond that will in all likelihood grow. The recycling of material used in manufacturing of jewellery like old jewellery and scraps is expected to develop for economic reasons. The demand for safe and healthy products is probably going to push for new regions of alloys, abandoning nickel, pursued by more tight regulations against other safe material like cadmium and lead, while research finds cobalt as another product. The significance to better service is likely to grow in finished jewellery segment about its mechanical attributes, tarnish resistance, quality, and finish and its extended longevity. The demand for customized jewellery is probably going to grow with the present rapid manufacturing technologies that increasingly facilitate the trend with optimal costs. The market is in steady pursuit of new colours and decorative effects. The unusual colours like purple gold is fast advancing while blue, brown, black are now commercially known with the rise of special alloys (known as inter metallic's) or coatings or surface treatment. The new advances in laser etching or surface or nanotechnology applications are developing that looks for harmonization with Hallmarking, regulation and finesse. A growing interest fast visible is in 'micro alloying' for stronger alloys. The 'bulk metallic glasses" is another frontier in the new alloy development which has attracted the jewellery manufactures. These alloys of complex compositions are rapidly cooled to keep up a non-crystalline state, which is a state of remarkable ductility that can be processed at low temperatures like plastics or glass and can be solidified back to normal alloy. These techniques offer incredible potential for alternative manufacturing processes with novel and unique design opportunities. On the processing side, investment casting will continue to improve to the challenges of CAD/CAM/RPT for more difficult shapes and finer wall thickness. The hollow casting technology however, is in its early form, offers exploration with RPT and direct casting of resin models. The improvement in investment machine technology and its consumables, mould rubber and investment powders are waiting in wings to happen. The CAD/CAM 3D printing technology can possibly improve model, pattern surface quality, process speed, and flexibility and improvement in use of machines. Again, the selective laser melting or sintering, offers exciting opportunities in the realm of design opportunities and its application in lightweight design opportunities from artistic perspective, however from engineering and economic front as a niche technology. The greater part of the technologies used in jewellery industry were initially developed in automobiles or aeronautic industry that was later embraced by the jewellery industry.

☐ Jewellery industry in 2020

The consumer appetite for jewellery that remains dampened by global recession after 2008 crisis shows up now to breathe fresh air. The industry is dynamic and fast growing and a few changes are in progress in both the consumer behaviour and the industry itself. The jewellery business persons should be alert and receptive to the trends and development else they risk themselves with situations that make them feel left behind by competitors that are more agile. It has been seen that the patterns that molded apparel industry for more than 30 years are very evident in the jewellery industry and are at a lot faster pace. The process of internationalization and consolidation, growth of branded products, remade distribution channel, hybrid consumption and fast fashion are fast catching the imagination of the consumers. The ten biggest jewellery group still captures an insignificant 12 percent of global market, and just two organizations in particular Cartier and Tiffany are in the brand ranking of best 100 worldwide brands. Whatever is left of the market comprises of strong national retail brands, for example, Christ in Germany, Chaw Tai Fook in China, and small and medium-sized companies that operate single-branch stores. It is normal that some flourishing national and local jewellery brands will join the rank of the best global brands (e.g. Swarovski). This will occur because of market consolidation in which International retail groups will in general acquire local jewelers.

The branded jewellery segment represents just 20 percent of jewellery market in 2003, however can possibly stretch around 30 to 40 percent by 2020. Right off the bat, this is because of the new money consumers who wear branded jewellery to flaunt their recently obtained wealth to 'old money' consumers, who favour treasure or estate jewellery. Besides, the emerging market consumers for whom established brands inspire trust, offers the feeling of

161

upgraded lifestyle. The young consumers will in general swing to brands as a means of self-expression and self-realization. The jewellery online sales in US is around 4 to 5 percent which is expected to grow to maximum count of 10 percent fine jewellery. The rationale that most buyers like to purchase expensive jewellery from brick and mortar stores often observed reliable, offers chance to touch and feel, and is driven by sensory factors, which is a defining factor in expensive item purchase. The fashion jewellery prospective players will have more shares of sales online of around 10 to 15 percent in US by 2020, which will have ripple effect around the world. The quantum of these sales is to originate from branded jewellery, a standardized product in which purchasers know precisely what they are getting. The manufacturers may use digital media platforms relaying information, molding brand personality, and customer relationships. The luxury customers will take part in online research before imminent purchase and may use web based social media for information and guidance. The single brand stores that have more control of their brands and contacts with customers, is probably going to make strides in regards to multi brand boutiques or departmental stores that have stagnated giving mono brands higher margins from consumers. The multi brand boutiques that offer select variety of brands and products with unique shopping experience can accomplish adequate margins when they operate on global scale. There is sign of increase in hybrid consumption, which is an inclination to trade up to top of the line and trade down to low end and no midpoint in jewellery purchases. In jewellery industry more individuals are trading up to standardized one-carat diamond engagement ring to three or four carats with more than five to six digit price tags. At the lower end, the department stores and retailers are pursuing price wars. The obvious boundaries between fine jewellery, which is portrayed by use of precious metal and stones, and fashion jewellery, which is normally made out of plated alloys and crystal stones, are gradually looking hazy. The fine jewellery that was once used as gift items are owned by themselves. It is expected by industry specialists that there are segments that will be defined by price points, brand positions, indifferent to purchase, and wearing occasions. The customer may choose to layer and mix high and low price points. This trend may push retailers of fine jewellery to present new product lines at reasonable prices for young or less affluent consumers, which offers an entry point into the brand. On the other hand, the fine jewellery players may play it solely in the high end and communicate through advertising, amplifying customer experience and customer service. The advancement of apparel industry could be a decent case for the jewellery industry development. What exact degree the two industries may reflect on each other remains to be seen if fast fashion catches the imagination of fashion jewellery (that attempts to be dynamic, globalized, and intensely competitive). The players who can envision and capitalize by the changing trend will stand to gain and remain ahead.

CONCLUSION

T

he canvass framed might lead us to believe that gold is a form of money since times immemorial, one which preserves wealth in times of financial volatility and act as a safe haven. In absence of gold standard, there is no way to protect savings from confiscation through inflation. Deficit spending is simply a scheme for the confiscation of wealth. In the Indian setting and its century old practices, gold is used in jewellery, which is visually alluring and pleasing to the wearer, a wearable wealth to consumers that draws attention when such a large number of individuals are employed in the industry and makes a living. The series of financial crisis indicates that dollar as fiat currency has confronted numerous tests because of excessive printing, but banking elites have quit discussing gold and chose openly to overlook it, yet themselves held on to it. The right balance between encouraging new growth and the path to social inclusion deserves a fresh look against restrictive policies. India, an immense market that values traditional gold jewellery, created by the skilled craftsmen need to graduate upward with unhindered supply of raw material, new enterprise, and re-skill part of its workforce in its endeavor of value addition, innovation, development of brands, making of clusters, common facility centres among others. India's love for gold originates from the gold jewellery consumption attached to its traditional culture in weddings, rituals, household ceremonies, festivals and a form of security "Streedhan", which is considered as most liquid and tradable investment for accumulation of wealth. In spite of changes presented in international policy combined with control measures, the appeal for gold jewellery consumption stay unaffected. The gold control policy, drawn to regulate gold supply to reduce smuggling, diminishes demand for gold and its price, could not move individuals away from gold. The liberalization of the economy with the annulment of the Gold Control Act 1990, have lend thrust to exports of jewellery from the country. The consolidation of domestic market marked removal of license that witnessed development prospects that were accelerated with normalization of Export Import policy initiatives by the successive governments. The presentation of GST has realized significant changes in the dynamics of tax administration that captures all the tax based on principle of place and supply of consumption, something much unknown to the industry. The understanding of gold fix mechanism by the jewelers and gold dealers may offer a clue to regular international price movements, which establishes a common transaction price for a large pool of purchase and sale order by the large participating banks. It is the price of gold in dollar that changes and said dollar price of gold. To get global viewpoint on gold, one needs to examine the cross currency rates that influence the physical gold market and paper gold market. Gold leasing and unallocated forwards are methods of manipulating gold price. Different players operate globally who has political and policy interests and they adopt these methods to suppress price of gold. There is no doubt demand for gold will continue to grow in future as domestic production in India is insignificant and supply from manufactured gold scraps not very meaningful. Therefore, rising demand has to be met from outside the country. Post independence, the gold control policy rotate around five primary goals, to wean individuals away from gold, to regulate supply of gold, reduce smuggling, to decrease demand for gold, and to lessen domestic price for gold. It may not be appropriate to regard gold jewellery as idle asset as it is also used as consumer durable. This makes it necessary to frame appropriate regulation for import, trading and market making in gold and related items to realize the potential of import liberalization. Again, the development of financial market in gold depends upon capital account convertibility, which may be a challenge. The tradition of adorning oneself with jewellery is 5000 years old in India. Indian women and jewelry have always formed a great combination. There is jewelry for almost all the parts of the body and is designed to match with the attire. The popularity of jewellery made out of stone, encrusted on metal, has grown more recently. The different kinds of jewellery that India produces are important to note that speak of its rich heritage and not something that happened only recently. It has to be seen how the traditional jewellery manufacturers protect and retain their customer base from the challenges from the branded jewellery segment. Jewellery manufacturing has progressively observed changes and improvement in technology. The trend and inclination in Europe and western world for white precious metal jewellery–silver, white gold, platinum palladium, with rise in prices of metals, has put pressure on improvement of alloys and assembling process with emphasis on lightweight jewellery. The computer-based technologies have come to influence market trends to life as new designs and products get into market faster. Despite these interventions, the customers of jewellery may show increasing enthusiasm for ethical use of materials that are safe and made in socially responsible environment.

It has become imperative for India to organize a superior business condition within the current scenario of incentives and subsidies to encourage youth to select business as a lifelong career choice. McKinsey and the International Finance Corporation have estimated the unmet need for credit for small and medium enterprises as up to US$2.5 trillion in developing countries and about US$3.5 trillion globally. The greatest challenge comes from the familiarity and awareness of different MSME schemes and plans in place. The schemes if offered under one umbrella may possibly energize the prospective entrepreneurs to increased productivity and efficiency. The Lean manufacturing techniques offer the MSMEs and SMEs sector for remarkable improvements in all sections of a manufacturing system. The unique form of wage payment in the gold jewellery sector that of wage-loss (or loss-wage) mechanism for determination and settlement of wage and disputes have largely isolated the industry to remain informal. The establishment of this model although has mitigated the industrial relations challenges, and in some measure also the dispute resolution over wages, prompting significant gain in production capabilities, yet very little gain has been witnessed in labor welfare, worker health, wellbeing of family, child labour, education and their general working conditions. Hallmarking, the oldest form of consumer protection, is essential to be done in India to determine accurately the proportion and purity of precious gold in the metal. The mark guarantees the fineness and purity of gold in jewellery that is set to establish renewal of trust and confidence of the consumers. Various channels of distribution have evolved in domestic as well as international trade. With the increasing awareness of the distribution system, techniques may be used in the sale of branded and customized jewellery.

The Beneficial Ownership in FATF standards may remain a key focus in the review of analogous countries and follow-up process. In the past, action was taken to facilitate transparency and access to beneficial ownership information on legal persons in a time bound manner coupled with its legal arrangements. The role of FATF as a global network body assesses compliance with beneficial ownership requirements, in the context of implementing AML/CFT measures. OECD again is an assessment body to assess compliance with beneficial ownership requirements in the context of transparency and exchange of information for tax purposes. The professional secrecy provision prevents identification of beneficial ownership of client account. It is believed that if the trade in precious metals and minerals are overseen legitimately, it provides opportunity for increased income. The basic principles of value added tax (VAT) designed to tax final consumption in jurisdiction where it occurs according to destination principal, has continued to spread across the world in the international trade of goods and services, in an increasingly globalised economy. The widespread consensus in the destination principle as international norm is sanctioned by WTO rules based on which India's GST framework is aligned (to match with the local needs and be representative). Another challenge faced by the exporters is the low level of research and development intensity and facilities. The research and development solutions might assist in enhancing product quality, reducing wastage, introducing new designs and concepts, and innovation in supply chain management and marketing. The gap between high-end machines and unskilled labour can be reduced with new R&D solutions.

The challenges that might come from white goods company of global stature and scale, including jewellery chains, making foray into Indian market have to be recognized. The rising market to digital content and services might offer new opportunities in abundance in the digital market space through the internet sales channels. These activities may call for application of artificial intelligence to read positive contents about the company and from the opinion leaders in the web-based social media space. The rating agencies have to play a crucial role to provide independent assessment on the creditworthiness of debt issuers. Today, the role played by Credit Rating Agencies has come into severe criticism and public scrutiny. The challenge that remains is the 'issuer-pays' revenue model of privately owned rating agencies that entail conflict of interest, and too many regulations that play out in the agencies effort of being credible and not to conservative in its approach to rating. The ownership of responsibility and accountability may be integral in valuing the investors interest in mind. The right to choose and pay a rating agency may always lead to the path of conflict of interest and oversight. The high barriers to entry of CRAs prevent competition that may protect the interest of the investors. A new consumer class is fast developing in the emerging markets that have their very own sense of difference and individuality. The companies may require distinctive value proposition to connect with each group and stand out in competitiveness. The electronics and white goods industries may drive the greater part of the global demand. The consumer class that evolved in the digital age has users in greater part from the emerging markets. The brands that build in trust that resonates may assume a significant role in deciding emerging market consumers. There may arise a need to position brands or auxiliary brands to target a thin consumer segment that offer more tailored value proposition. To maximize and interface with consumer segment, it may require creation of a range of brands and secondary or associate brands to amplify on their brands range. The jewellery market in emerging markets (BRICS) is ready to grow and alter the economics of manufacturing. In the area of designs in jewellery, fashion and luxury goods, Italy and Europe may continue as market leaders. The significance to better service is likely to grow in finished jewellery segment about its mechanical attributes, tarnish resistance, quality, and finish and its extended longevity. The economic prospect of the emerging markets is poised for growth provided it is able to balance its economic priorities as opposed to structural challenges and recessionary pressures sweeping the globe. A carefully crafted financial and monetary policies and its regulation might decide the future of Indian industries in realizing its full potential particularly of those sectors like inputs in jewellery, which is import based. A large number of workers, particularly in the informal sector, are not covered by core labour laws and social insurance programs which is desired. There is a need to incentivize firms to create jobs, access education and provide early vocational training. Trade policies are an instrument of economic and social development for overall economic growth and social change. Too much of politics with little real work and serious dialogue in turbulent times lead us nowhere. Despite hurdles and difficulties, belief in hard thinking, right actions and tough decisions might destine India to be a major powerhouse of the global economy. "Patience is power. Patience is not an absence of action; rather it is timing; it waits on the right time to act, for the right principles and in the right way.", Fulton J. Sheen.

171

ABBREVIATIONS

AML	Anti Money Laundering
AEI	Automatic Exchange of Information
BIS	Bank for International Settlement
BCD	Basic Customs Duty
BPLR	Benchmark Prime Lending Rate
BRICS	Brazil Russia India China South Africa
BSM	Buyer Seller Meet
CAD	Capital Account Deficit
CBGA	Central Bank Gold Agreement
CEBC	Central Board of Excise and Customs
CFT	Combating Financing of Terrorism
COMEX	Commodity Exchange
CFC	Common Facility Centre
CAD	Computer Aided Design
CAM	Computer Aided Manufacturing

CGTMSE	Credit Guarantee Fund Trust for Micro and Small Enterprise
CLCSS	Credit Linked Capital Subsidy Scheme
CRA	Credit Rating Agency
CDD	Customer Due Diligence
DOBOD	Department of Banking Operation and Development
DNFBP	Designated Non Financial Business and Profession
DGFT	Directorate General of Foreign Trade
DIC	District Industries Centre
DDS	Duty Drawback Scheme
DTA	Duty Tariff Area
EIC	Economic Intelligence Unit
EDI	Electronic Data Interchange
ED	Enforcement Directorate
ESMA	European Securities and Market Authorities
ETF	Exchange Traded Fund
EXIM	Export Import
EPZ	Export Processing Zone

FICCI	Federation of Indian Chamber of Commerce and Industries
FIU	Financial Intelligence Unit
FT	Financing Terrorism
FATF	Foreign Action Task Force
FIRC	Foreign Exchange Inward Remittance Certificate
FERA	Foreign Exchange Regulation Act
FTP	Foreign Trade Policy
FOB	Free on Board
GJEPC	Gem and Jewellery Export Promotion Council
GSI	Geological Survey Of India
GCA	Gold Control Act
GDS	Gold Deposit Scheme
GMC	Gold Management Corporation
GST	Goods and Services Tax
GOI	Government of India
GDP	Gross Domestic Product
HHEC	Handloom and Handicraft Export Promotion Council

HSN	Harmonized System of Nomenclature
IBM	Indian Bureau of Mines
ILFS	Infrastructure Lease and Financial Services
IRDA	Insurance Regulatory Development Authority
IGST	Integrated Goods and Services Tax
IPR	Intellectual Property Right
IMF	International Monetary Fund
IOSCO	International Organization of Securities Commission
ITC	International Trade Centre
ITC	Input Tax Credit
KPCS	Kimberly Process Certificate Scheme
LEA	Law Enforcement Agency
LMT	Lean Manufacturing Technology
LPS	Lean Production System
LBMA	London Bullion Market Association
LGFM	London Gold Fix Mechanism
LGFP	London Gold Fix Price

LGMF	London Gold Market Fix
MAI	Market Access Initiative
MDA	Market Development Assistance
MSE-CDP	Micro Small Enterprise Cluster Development Program
MSME	Micro Small Medium Enterprise
MUDRA	Micro Units Development and Reliance Agency Limited
MMTC	Mineral & Metal Trading Corporation
MVA	Most Valuable Asset
NDPS	Narcotic Drugs and Psychotropic Substance
NMCP	National Manufacturing Competitiveness Program
NMIU	National Monitoring and Implementing Unit
NSDC	National Skill Development Council
NFE	Net Foreign Exchange
NPA	Non Performing Asset
NRS	Non Registered Supplier
OGL	Open General License
OECD	Organization for Economic Cooperation and

Development

PSSA	Payment and Settlement Systems Act
PFRDA	Pension Fund Regulatory Development Authority
PMS	Precious Metals and Stones
PMLA	Prevention of Money Laundering Act
PSU	Public Sector Unit
RPT	Rapid Prototyping Technology
REP	Replenishment
RBI	Reserve Bank Of India
RCM	Reverse Charge Mechanism
RBA	Risk Based Approach
SEEPZ	Santacruz Electronic Export Processing Zone
SEBI	Securities and Exchange Board of India
SEC	Security Exchange Commission
SCO	Shanghai Cooperation Organization
SIDBI	Small Industries Development Bank Of India
SEZ	Special Economic Zone

SIL	Special Imprest License
SPV	Special Purpose Vehicle
STC	State Trading Corporation
STR	Suspicious Transaction Report
TBML	Trade Based Money Laundering
UN	United Nation
UNCTAD	United Nation Culture Trade and Development
UAPA	Unlawful Activities Prevention Act
VAT	Value Added Tax
WEEE	Waste Electrical and Electronic Equipment
WGC	World Gold Council
WTO	World Trade Organization
WW1	World War 1
WW2	World War 2

REFERENCES

Introduction

- In Gold we trust 2016, Incrementum AG, June 2016.

- Why India needs a Gold Policy, FICCI-World Gold Council Report.

- The overseeing of Globalization-Dr. Joseph Stiglitz

- Annual Report: 2016-17, MOC, GOI.

- IMF Managing Director's Global Policy Agenda-A more inclusive and resilient global economy, April 2017.

- Working Paper IMF : Background and issues for Congress, Martin A. Weiss, July 2014.

- Priorities for Structural reforms in G20 countries, July, 2016.

- Normalization of Global Financial Conditions: The implication of Brazil, by Troy Matheson, June 2015.

- How to reduce climate change using new IMF Special Drawing Rights-World Future Council

- A Hundred Small Steps Report of the Committee on Financial Sector Reforms-Dr. Raghu Rajan, Planning Commission of India 2009.

- End of an Epoch: Britain's Withdrawal from the Gold Standard -Michael Kitson, UOC, 2012.

- The direct economic impact of gold - A PWC report for WGC 2013.

Chapter 1

- The Gold Standard, Deflation, and Financial Crisis in the Great Depression: An International Comparison Ben Bernanke and Harold James, 1991.

- Gold and the divergent path of global central bank holdings- Michael Lewis 2014.

- Gold Fundamental Report, KMD of NCDEX , Feb 2012.

- Containing the Demand for Gold by Dr. C. Rangarajan, Chairman, Economic Advisory Council to the Prime Minister, May 15, 2013.

- Reviving and Accelerating India's Exports: Policy Issues and Suggestions By H.A.C. Prasad, Ministry of Finance, GOI. 2017.

- "All that glitters is Gold: India Jewellery Review 2013" a study by AT Kearney and FICCI.

- A short history of international currencies by Christopher Weber.

- An introduction to the Indian Gold Market by Nigel Deserbrock, Grendon International Research.

- IMF Working Paper " Breaking through the zero lower bound" by Ruchir Agarwal and Miles Kimball.

- Gold Fundamental Report 2012 – Ashwin D. Bahate

- Sector Leadership plan for Gem & Jewellery Industry, W.B-A report of KPMG, N. Delhi.

- What a difference 10 years can make, The LBMA (LPPM) Precious metals conference, Sept, 2011.

- Changing trends: Gems & Jewellery Industry, ONICRA, Nov 2013.

- A Case for Gold- A minority report of the US Gold commission: Rep. Ron Paul.

- Currency Wars : James Rickard
- The new case for Gold : James Rickard
- Essays on the Great Depression : Ben S. Bernanke
- The Shock Doctrine: Naomi Klein
- Who Rules The World : Noam Chomsky
- www.ibma.org.uk
- www.gold.org
- www.kitco.com
- www.treasury.gov
- www.finmin.nic.in
- www.rbi.org.in
- http://goldnews.bullionvault.com

Chapter 2

- Proceedings of the Jewellery technology forum : 2014.
- "The gold industry through technology and innovation" Monte Grotto, Italy 2004.
- "Lean Manufacturing and theory of constraints principles in the jewellery manufacturing environment" A. Hill, Proceedings of the 15th Santa Fe Symposium, 2001.
- "The application of Lean Manufacturing and theory of constraints principles in jewellery manufacturing operations" Gold Technology, Spring 2002, p. 3-12.
- "Global trends and innovation in the jewellery sector" B. Biagi, JTF 2006.

- "Jewellery identity project", JTF 2008.

- "Fine Jewellery in an era of communication", JTF 2009.

- Global trends and innovation in Jewellery: reflections and predictions", JTF 2010.

- "Rapid Manufacturing and precious metals" J.T. Strauss, Santa Fe Symposium, 2009.

- "Responsible manufacturing : Being Green and Ethical in the Jewellery sector" C.W. Corti, JTF 2011.

- "Quality in the jewellery industry beyond 2000: A review of progress 1998-2007 " Christopher Corti, Santa Fe Symposium, JTF 2014.

- G20 Communiqué, Finance Ministers and Central Bank Governors, March 2018, Buenos Aires, Argentina.

- Report on conditions of work and promotion of livelihoods in the Unorganized sector-National Commission for Enterprises in the organized sector, N. Delhi.

- Wage dispersion and the loss wage model: Sukanta Saha, IJHSS

- Indian Economic Outlook 2018, Deloitte.

- Introduction to credit rating agencies. A presentation of
  Educen FSI.

- FATF business bulletin report, March 2018.

- Exchange of Information on Request, OECD 2016-20.

- Enhancing the effectiveness of external support in building tax capacity in developing countries- IMF, OECD, UN, WBG for G-20 Ministers.

- Whither monetary and financial stability, the implications of evolving policy regimes- Claudio Borio and William White 2004.

- G-20 Leaders Communiqué, Brisbane Summit, November, 2014.

- FATF Report to G-20 on Beneficial Ownership, September 2016.

- Goods and Services Tax in India, Taking stock and setting expectations-A study by ASSOCHAM and Deloitte 2015.

- Action Plan on BEPS-OECD publication 2013.

- Priorities of the 2017 G20 Summit, Hamburg, Germany 2017.

- Implementing AML/CFT measures in Precious Minerals sector: Preventing crime while increasing revenue-Emanuel Mathais & Bert Feys, IMF legal department, August 2014.

- Overview of India's export performance: Trends & Drivers, Working Paper no. 363, Shameek Mukherjee, Sahana Mukherjee, IIM, Bangalore.

- G-20 Brisbane Anti Corruption update, 2014.

- G-20 Leader's Communique Antalaya, Summit, Turkey, 2015.

- Exchange of Information on Request-Handbook for peer reviews 2016-2020, OECD publication.

- International tax challenges for Asia and the G-20: Competition and Cordination, Prof. Miranda Stewart.

- International VAT/GST Guidelines, OECD Report Nov 2015.

- RBA Guidance for Dealers in precious metals and stones- FATF/OECD 2008.

- Recovery and refining of Gold jewellery scraps and wastes by C.W. Corti, Director, International technology, WGC, London, U.K.

- www.knonoune.com

- www.marketing.com

- www.investopedia.com/terms/d/distribution-channel.asp

Chapter 3

- OECD Economic surveys India, Feb 2017.

- Winning the $30 trillion decathlon, McKinsey & Co. 2012.

- Perspectives on retail and consumer goods, no. 2, Winter 2013-14, Mc Kinsey & Co. report.

- NSDC Report 2012, 2013-2017.

- Global powers of retailing 2018-Retail trends, A report of Deloitte Touche Tohmatsu Limited.

- Conclusion

- Ibid.

- www.goldnrajguru.com

ABOUT THE AUTHOR

Shantanu Rajguru is a widely acknowledged industry expert whose decades of experience manifests itself in this book. He is a graduate in Physics, Masters in Business Management from University of Calcutta, a Post graduate diploma in Foreign trade, has served for more than a decade in The Gem and Jewellery Export Promotion Council as Director, Eastern Region. He served the Textile industries for a decade and was with Indian Rayon and Churchgate, Nigeria in responsible positions. He served as advisor to textile EOUs, held teaching posts in management at IIEM, Kolkata, visiting faculties at IIFT, Kolkata, MSME, GOI, Kolkata, and as a jury in NIFT, Kolkata. His career spanned 27 years and has travelled extensively within India and abroad. He is now a freelance Advisor and Consultant to the industry and involved in projects close to his heart. He serves as Advisor to a leading publication house and industry organizations in the country. He has interest in international trade and business practices, international economics, geopolitics and world order. He is an author, writes articles and runs a blog : www. goldnrajguru.com.

www.ingramcontent.com/pod-product-compliance
Lightning Source LLC
Chambersburg PA
CBHW072137170526
45158CB00004BA/1404

* 9 7 8 1 0 9 2 9 1 3 9 4 2 *